Prayers For My Children

PRAYERS FOR MY CHILDREN

A Daily Guide to Praying Scripture For Your Children

LAURA SHOOK

Permissions

ISBN: 1537591916
ISBN 13: 9781537591919
Library of Congress Control Number: 2016919282
CreateSpace Independent Publishing Platform
North Charleston, South Carolina

PRAYERS FOR MY CHILDREN

FROM THE MOMENT I first became a parent, my strongest desire has been for my children to know and love God. I believe one of the main responsibilities God has given to me, as a parent, is to pray for my children. I know that God listens and responds to prayer and I count it a great honor and privilege to bring my children before Him on a daily basis. The Bible teaches us to be persistent in prayer. I want God to daily hear the names and needs of my children before him. I can think of no better words to pray than the words of the Bible. In 2014 I started keeping a journal of the Scriptures I was praying over my children as a tool to ensure my consistency in prayer, and as a reminder of the things I had asked God to do in the lives of each of my children. My hope is that this small prayer journal will also be a tool for you, encouraging you to pray for your children, reminding you of the goodness and faithfulness of God, and showing you the power of a praying parent as you look back over your prayers to see the miracles that have taken place as you prayed.

JANUARY 1

"For the Lord watches over the way of the righteous..."

PSALM 1:6 (NIV)

Lord, I pray that each of my children would daily choose righteousness. As they do, I thank you for watching over their ways. Thank you that you never close your eyes in sleep and you never take your eye off of them.

JANUARY 2

"Serve the Lord with reverent fear..."

PSALM 2:11 (NLT)

I pray that each of my children would daily serve you. I pray they would live in awe of your majesty. I pray their love for you would lead them to live lives of service.

JANUARY 3

"But you, Lord, are a shield around me; my glory, the One who lifts my head high."

PSALM 3:3 (NIV)

Thank you that you are a shield around each of my children. Thank you that you can be trusted to encourage each one and lift their heads high on difficult days.

JANUARY 4

"Know that the Lord has set apart his faithful servant for himself; the Lord hears when I call to him."

PSALM 4:3 (NIV)

Thank you for setting each of my children apart for your purposes. Thank you for listening when they call to you. Please open their hearts to hear when you call to them. I pray they would daily respond in obedience to your voice.

JANUARY 5

"In the morning, Lord, you hear my voice; in the morning I lay my requests before you and wait expectantly."

PSALM 5:3 (NIV)

I pray each of my children would daily bring their requests to you. I pray they would learn early in life to wait expectantly for you, trusting that you will meet their every need.

JANUARY 6

"Turn, Lord, and deliver me; save me because of your unfailing love."

PSALM 6:4 (NIV)

Thank you for saving each of my children. Thank you that your love for them is unfailing. Thank you for always turning to them when they call on you, and that you are faithful to deliver them.

JANUARY 7

"My shield is God Most High, who saves the upright in heart."

PSALM 7:10 (NIV)

I pray each of my children would recognize you as God Most High. I pray each one would know you as Savior. Teach them to live upright in heart.

JANUARY 8

" You have taught children and babies to sing praises to you..."

PSALM 8:2 (NCV)

Lord, I pray that from the lips of my children, and my grandchildren, and their children, that you would receive praise. I pray each one would daily praise your Holy name.

JANUARY 9

"I will praise you, Lord, with all my heart; I will tell of all the marvelous things you have done. I will be filled with joy because of you. I will sing praises to your name, O Most High."

PSALM 9:1-2 (NLT)

Lord, I pray that each of my children would use their voices to tell others about you – who you are and what you do. I pray they would come to recognize that you are the "Most High" and that you are above every other thing. I pray they would find joy in their relationship with you on a daily basis.

JANUARY 10

"In his pride the wicked man does not seek him; in all his thoughts there is no room for God."

PSALM 10:4 (NIV)

Lord, I pray each of my children would daily seek you. Please protect them from the sin of pride; from thinking they don't need you. Let them make room in their thoughts for you.

JANUARY 11

"In the Lord I take refuge."

PSALM 11:1 (NIV)

Lord, I pray each of my children will take refuge in you always. I pray they will see and experience you as a safe place. I pray they will understand your unconditional love and acceptance of them and that this understanding will lead them to always run to you.

JANUARY 12

"And the words of the Lord are flawless."

PSALM 12:6 (NIV)

Thank you that your words are flawless. I pray my children will see the truth of your Word, and that they would live their lives according to your Word. I pray each one would see Scripture as your divine Word. I pray that they would memorize your words and hide them in their hearts so that at the moment they need them they will be there. I pray you would develop in each of them a deep love for your Word.

JANUARY 13

"But I trust in your unfailing love; my heart rejoices in your salvation. I will sing to the Lord, for he has been good to me."

PSALM 13:5-6 (NIV)

Lord, I pray my children would always trust in your unfailing love, and that their hearts would be full of joy knowing your salvation. I pray they would recognize all the ways you are good to them, and it would cause them to sing, write, and tell of your goodness. Thank you that you are good to them, that you have saved them, that your love will never fail them. Open their eyes to see that truth.

JANUARY 14

"The Lord looks down from heaven on the sons of men to see if there are any who understand, any who seek God."

PSALM 14:2 (NASB)

Lord, I thank you that you are looking down at my children. I pray they will be found to be among those who seek you. I pray they will daily seek you in the Scripture, in their thoughts and in meditation. I pray they will seek you in the faces of people, and in the beauty around them. Open their eyes to your constant presence. Please use the circumstances of their life to compel them to seek you today.

JANUARY 15

"Lord, who may dwell in your sanctuary? Who may live on your holy hill? He whose walk is blameless and who does what is righteous."

PSALM 15:1-2 (NIV)

Thank you for providing a place for my children in your presence. Please open their eyes to see your way, and help them daily choose to do what is righteous. I pray righteousness would not just be something that they think about, talk about, theorize about, sing about, or discuss; but that it would be action in their lives. I pray each of them would be known for righteousness.

JANUARY 16

"And I have said, 'Only you are my Lord! Every good thing that I have is a gift from you.'"

PSALM 16:2 (CEV)

I pray each of my children would say, "Only You are my Lord" today and every day of their lives. I pray in every relationship and every circumstance they would recognize and honor you as their Lord. I pray their marriages would reflect the fact that they have made you Lord of their lives. I pray each one would recognize that every good thing in their life, no matter what it is, is a gift from you. I pray that they would see your goodness today and be reminded of your love for them. Please develop goodness in their character so they can be reflection of you to the world. Thank you for how you love my children.

JANUARY 17

"My steps have held to your paths; my feet have not slipped."

PSALM 17:5 (NIV)

Lord, I know that you designed and planned a path for each of my children from the very beginning. You know where they've been, where they are, and where they're headed. Thank you that I don't have to worry about it because you've already got it figured out. I pray each day they would look to you for guidance and they would choose to follow you each step along the way. I pray their feet would not slip and they would hold to your path. Lord, any time they step out of your plan, I ask you to gently call them back. Help them always to see your way and choose it.

JANUARY 18

"He reached down from on high and took hold of me, he drew me out of deep waters. He rescued me from my powerful enemy."

PSALM 18:16-17 (NLT)

Lord, thank you that you have reached down and taken hold of each of my children. Thank you that I can rest in the knowledge that they are in your hand. Thank you that nothing can take them from your hand. I pray when they find themselves in deep water that they would look to you to draw them out. I thank you that you always rescue them from the enemy. I pray that you would block every plan of the enemy that would try to come into their lives; and that you would accomplish every good plan you have for each of their lives.

JANUARY 19

"Keep your servant also from willful sins, may they not rule over me."

PSALM 19:13 (NIV)

Lord, please keep my children from willful sins today. Let them choose against what they know to be wrong. I pray they would spend time in your Word so they know your truth and are able to discern what is sin. Convict them of sin and of truth today. I pray no sin or sinful choice will ever rule over them. Please protect them from any form of addiction including drugs, alcohol, pornography, or any other thing that would try to rule over them. Let them walk in the light.

JANUARY 20

"May he give you the desire of your heart and make all your plans succeed."

PSALM 20:4 (NIV)

I pray each of my children would delight in you daily, and in so doing that you would bless them with the fulfillment of their dreams. I pray you would make all their plans succeed, and that everything they do would bring glory and honor to you. Thank you for placing your dreams in them. Thank you for what you are doing in and through each of their lives.

JANUARY 21

"Surely you have granted him unending blessings and made him glad with the joy of your presence."

PSALM 21:6 (NIV)

Thank you that you freely pour your blessings on my children. Thank you that there is no end to those blessings. Thank you that you bless each of my children with joy in your presence. I pray wherever they are and whatever they are doing today, their eyes would be opened to your presence. Let knowledge of your presence fill them with joy.

JANUARY 22

"I will declare your name to my brothers; in the congregation I will praise you."

PSALM 22:22 (ESV)

I pray each of my children would be counted among those who declare your name. I pray they would declare your name to their family members, to their friends, to those they work with and those they go to school with. I pray they would proclaim your name to their neighbors and to each person they encounter today. I pray each of my children would be an active, faithful member of a Bible-believing congregation and they would praise you together with their church. I ask you to bring other believers into their lives to be their friends and to walk through life with them. Give each of them a desire to be involved in church, and a deep hunger for you and your kingdom.

JANUARY 23

"Yes, goodness and faithful love will pursue me all the days of my life..."

PSALM 23:6 (CEB)

Thank you, Lord, that your goodness and faithful love pursue each of my children. Thank you that you will continue this pursuit all the days of their life. Thank you that you are the pursuer; no matter what they do or where they go, you will be pursuing them. Thank you that they can't outrun you. They can never get too far away from you or out of your sight. Thank you that you never give up, you never stop pursuing. I pray that each of them would become pursuers of men for your kingdom; that they would be like you. Wherever they live, whatever they do, whomever they talk to or hang out with, shine through them so that the world sees you.

JANUARY 24

"Who is the King of Glory? The Lord, strong and mighty, the Lord, invincible in battle."

PSALM 24:8 (NIV)

Please glorify yourself as King in the life of each of my children. I pray whatever battles they face today, whether it be outside sources or thoughts in their own minds, that you would show yourself to be strong and mighty on their behalf. Let no enemy defeat them. Please be strong, mighty, and invincible on behalf of each of them every day of their lives.

JANUARY 25

"Lead me by your truth and teach me, for you are the God who saves me. All day long I put my hope in you."

PSALM 25:5 (NLT)

I pray you would lead each of my children by your truth today. As you lead, I pray they would humble themselves and choose to follow. Help each one recognize your voice and your leading. Please examine their hearts and minds and teach them the things you want them to know. Thank you that they can always hope in you because you are faithful.

JANUARY 26

"I see your love, and I live by your truth."

PSALM 26:3 (NCV)

I pray my children would see your love every day. Open their eyes to your love; help them to recognize it in the people and circumstances around them. Please lead them, teach them, and discipline them out of love. I pray every day you would reveal your truth to them and that they would choose to live by your truth.

JANUARY 27

"The Lord is my light and the one who saves me. So why should I fear anyone? The Lord protects my life. So why should I be afraid?"

PSALM 27:1 (NCV)

Thank you that you are the one who saves my children. I pray whenever they face dark days they would look to you as their light. Please break any chains of fear that would try to bind them or keep them from accomplishing their dreams and the purpose for which you created them. Thank you for protecting their lives. Let them live in confidence and act with courage, fearless for your Kingdom.

JANUARY 28

"I am very happy and I praise him with my song."

PSALM 28:7 (NCV)

I pray each of my children would experience happiness in your presence on a daily basis. I pray each one would praise you using the talents and gifts you have given to them; and that they would use those gifts to honor and glorify you. I pray you would put a song in their hearts day and night; and that you would sing over them. I pray you would protect them from depression. Heal any thoughts or emotions that would entrap them and take away their joy. Heal any physical issues that would lead to depression.

January 29

"The Lord reigns as King forever."

Psalm 29:10 (NLT)

I praise you because you reign as King forever. I pray each of my children would recognize that truth. I pray each one would worship you as the reigning King, and choose to submit themselves to your reign in their lives. I pray every decision they make would be made in light of the fact that you are King. Show them your glory today.

January 30

"I will praise you, Lord, for you have saved me from my enemies. You refuse to let them triumph over me."

Psalm 30:1 (TLB)

I praise you, Lord, for you have saved my children from their enemies; and you refuse to let their enemies triumph over them. Thank you that you know who and what their enemies are; and you are always watching out for them and protecting them. Thank you that you love them enough to do so.

JANUARY 31

"My future is in your hands."

PSALM 31:15 (NLT)

Lord, I thank you that the future of each of my children is in your hands. Thank you that I can trust you and I don't have to worry about my children. You know every detail of their future, and you are prepared to walk through the future with them. Help me to trust you with each child.

FEBRUARY 1

"I said to myself, 'I will confess my rebellion to the Lord.' And you forgave me! All my guilt is gone."

PSALM 32:5 (NLT)

I pray each of my children would be convicted of sin and rebellion and they would confess it to you. Thank you that you always stand ready to forgive them. Thank you that you remove their guilt. I pray you would set them free from any false guilt that the enemy would try to put on them. I pray each time they sin, they would immediately be aware of it and make it right with you. Make them sensitive to your Spirit working in their lives.

FEBRUARY 2

"He loves whatever is just and good..."

PSALM 33:5 (NLT)

I praise you, Lord, because you love whatever is just and good. I pray each of my children would love whatever is just and good, just like you. Let this characterize their lives and be the thing that they are known for.

FEBRUARY 3

"The righteous person faces many troubles, but the Lord comes to the rescue each time."

PSALM 34:19 (NLT)

Thank you, Lord, that you are the rescuer of my children, and I am not. Thank you that you come to their rescue every single time they face trouble, no matter what that trouble may be. I pray that in the midst of trouble each of my children would look to you; and that they would be aware of your presence working in their lives. Please use the troubles they face to make them more like you, and to develop strength in their character. Use the troubles in their lives to show others your glory.

FEBRUARY 4

**"O Lord, oppose those who oppose me. Fight those who
fight against me."**

PSALM 35:1 (NLT)

Thank you that you are aware of the spiritual forces that would try to fight against each of my children. I ask you to oppose those forces and prevent them from interfering in their lives. I ask you to fight against any spiritual force that would engage in battle against any of my children. Open their eyes to see the true nature of their enemies and teach them to be overcomers as they walk in step with you.

FEBRUARY 5

**"For you are the fountain of life, the light by which
we see."**

PSALM 36:9 (NLT)

Thank you, Lord, that you give life to each of my children. I ask you to continue to pour life on them. Thank you that you flood their lives with light. I pray that they would live and move within your light, and that they would daily look to you for life and light.

FEBRUARY 6

"Be still in the presence of the Lord, and wait patiently for him to act."

PSALM 37:7 (NLT)

I pray each of my children would learn to trust you so completely they are able to be still in your presence. I pray each one would know you so intimately that they are able to patiently wait for you to act no matter the circumstances. I pray they would see your glory in action as they wait for you.

FEBRUARY 7

"You know what I long for, Lord; you hear my every sigh."

PSALM 38:9 (NLT)

Thank you that you hear and know the longing of the hearts of each of my children. Thank you that you have placed your desires in them. Please fulfill those desires in and through them. Thank you that you hear their every sigh. On those days when they are weary, overwhelmed, or discouraged, please hold them close and comfort them. Let them feel your presence in those moments and remember that you hear them even when no one else does.

FEBRUARY 8

"I said to myself, 'I will watch what I do and not sin in what I say.'"

PSALM 39:1 (NLT)

I pray each of my children would always be careful to watch what they are doing so that their actions would reflect their relationship with you. I pray each one would choose not to sin with their words. Teach them to guard their tongues, to be slow to speak, and to communicate truth and love with their words. I pray that you would temper their words, their tone, and their expressions so that the world would see and hear you in them.

FEBRUARY 9

"I take joy in doing your will, my God, for your instructions are written on my heart."

PSALM 40:8 (NLT)

Thank you, Lord, for writing your instructions on the hearts of each of my children. I pray each one would take joy in doing your will today, and every day of their life. I pray whenever they step out of your will that they would be immediately and keenly aware of that misstep; and that they would choose to step back into your will quickly.

FEBRUARY 10

**"You always heal them and restore their strength when
they are sick."**

PSALM 41:3 (CEV)

Thank you that you heal each of my children. Thank you that you always
restore their strength. I ask you to heal any physical, emotional, or spiritual
sickness that they may have over the course of their lifetime. Please protect
them from any chronic diseases taking hold in their bodies. Please protect
them from mental illness. Please protect and heal any cancers that would try
to invade, or any type of pathogen that would try to establish itself in their
bodies.

FEBRUARY 11

**"Why am I discouraged? Why am I restless? I trust
you! And I will praise you again because you help me
and you are my God"**

PSALM 42:5 (CEV)

I pray whenever my children feel discouraged that they would trust you and
praise you, knowing that you will help them. I pray when they feel restless
that they would trust you and praise you knowing that you are their God.

FEBRUARY 12

"Send your light and your truth to guide me."

PSALM 43:3 (CEV)

Please send your light and your truth to guide my children. Remove anything from their lives or their minds that would keep them from seeing your light and truth, or keep them from walking in your light and truth today.

FEBRUARY 13

"Our hearts haven't turned away from you and we haven't stopped following you."

PSALM 44:18 (NCV)

I pray none of my children will ever turn away from you or stop following you. Please draw each one deeper and closer to you on a daily basis. When they have the choice to turn from you, please give them the wisdom, courage, and strength to continue following you.

FEBRUARY 14

"I will bring honor to your name in every generation. Therefore the nations will praise you forever and ever."

PSALM 45:17 (NLT)

I pray each of my children would bring honor to you among their generation. I pray they would help lead their generation to you. Let them be the ones to lead the way. Please use them to lead the nations to praise you forever and ever.

FEBRUARY 15

"So we will not fear…"

PSALM 46:2 (NLT)

Thank you, Lord; that my children have no reason to fear. I pray each of them would learn this truth early in life and they would hold on to it daily. Help them to turn every fearful or anxious thought into prayer.

FEBRUARY 16

"Sing praises to God, sing praises; sing praises to our King, sing praises!"

PSALM 47:6 (NLT)

I pray each of my children would recognize you as the one true King and that they would sing praises to you daily. I ask you to do whatever it takes in each of their lives to bring them to a place where they gladly choose to humble themselves before you.

FEBRUARY 17

"Your strong right hand is filled with victory."

PSALM 48:10 (NLT)

Thank you that your strong right hand is filled with victory. I pray each of my children would experience and live in your victory today and every day of their lives. Wherever and whenever they need victory in the course of their life, please step in and provide it. Let them always look to you for victory.

FEBRUARY 18

"But as for me, God will redeem my life."

PSALM 49:15 (NLT)

Thank you for being the redeemer of my children. Please restore each one to the original purpose for which you created them. Please use each one for your divine purpose.

FEBRUARY 19

"Make thankfulness your sacrifice to God,"

PSALM 50:14 (NLT)

I pray each of my children would daily give you the sacrifice of thankfulness. Please develop in each of them an attitude of daily thankfulness. I pray they would freely express their thankfulness and they would always remember to do so. I pray they would be known as grateful people by all who come in contact with them. Teach them gratitude, let them learn it early in life, and let them see the benefits of a thankful heart.

February 20

"...make me willing to obey you."

Psalm 51:12 (NLT)

I pray each of my children would know and understand the blessing of obedience. I pray their first response to your Spirit and your Word would be obedience. When obedience seems to be a difficult choice, please give them the wisdom, courage, and strength needed to make that choice.

February 21

"Don't you realize God's justice continues forever?"

Psalm 52:1 (NLT)

I pray each of my children would realize that God's justice continues forever and that this knowledge would give them hope. I pray as they see and experience the injustice of our world they would not become cynical but they would hope in you, knowing you will come again and make all things new. I pray each one would recognize you are the only source of lasting justice.

FEBRUARY 22

"When God restores his people…"

PSALM 53:6 (NLT)

I pray each of my children would realize you are the God of restoration. When people or situations in their lives feel hopeless I pray they would remember that you always restore your people. It's not a question of if, but only a question of when. I pray you would give them hope and patience as they wait for your restoration; and you would give them wisdom to know their part in that restoration.

FEBRUARY 23

"The Lord keeps me alive."

PSALM 54:4 (NLT)

Thank you that you keep my children alive. Thank you that you numbered and planned every day of each of their lives before the foundation of the world. Thank you that nothing can take them out of your hand. Thank you that they will live out each day you ordained for them.

FEBRUARY 24

"…he will never let the righteous be shaken."

PSALM 55:22 (NIV)

Thank you that as my children walk with you, you won't allow them to be shaken. Help each of them to see and stand in that truth no matter the circumstances of their lives. Please call them to righteousness on a daily basis. Give them wisdom to build their lives upon you – their strong foundation.

FEBRUARY 25

"When I am afraid I put my trust in you."

PSALM 56:3 (NIV)

Thank you that my children can trust you in times when they are afraid. I pray that each one would see you as trustworthy. When fears arise I pray they would immediately choose to put their trust in you. I pray that as they trust you they would experience supernatural peace, and they would see your power at work in the situation. Thank you for caring for each of my children.

February 26

"I cry out to God Most High, to God who will fulfill his purpose for me."

Psalm 57:2 (NLT)

Thank you, Lord, that you have a life purpose for each of my children. And thank you that you are and you will fulfill that purpose in their lives. I pray each one would know and feel a sense of purpose and that they would live in that purpose daily. Use them for your kingdom and your glory.

February 27

"Make their weapons useless in their hands."

Psalm 58:7 (NLT)

I pray any weapon the enemy would try to use against my children would be made useless by your power; any temptation to sin would be made powerless in their lives; any stronghold the enemy tries to establish in their lives would be thwarted; any lies the enemy would whisper to their hearts and minds would fall useless to the ground.

FEBRUARY 28

"In his unfailing love, my God will stand with me."

PSALM 59:10 (NLT)

Thank you for this beautiful promise! Thank you that my children can rest in this truth. Thank you that your presence in their lives is not dependent on their actions, beliefs, successes, or failures; but is wholly dependent on your unfailing love. Thank you they can rest in the fact that your love has never failed nor will it ever fail. Thank you that you are standing with each of my children.

MARCH 1

"With God's help we will do mighty things, for he will trample down our foes."

PSALM 60:12 (NLT)

Thank you, Lord, that you will help each of my children to do great things. I ask you to trample down their foes today, and every day of their lives. Help each one to recognize you at work in their lives and to step into your plans.

MARCH 2

"You have given me an inheritance reserved for those who fear your name."

PSALM 61:5 (NLT)

Thank you for designing an inheritance for each of my children. Thank you for providing this inheritance out of the riches of your glory. Thank you there is nothing they will ever need for which you haven't already made provision. I pray each of them would know you so completely that they would understand and rely on the inheritance you provide for them, finding peace and joy in your provision.

MARCH 3

"My victory and honor come from God alone."

PSALM 62:7 (NLT)

I pray each of my children would recognize you are their source of victory and honor. I pray every time they experience success, or are honored for an accomplishment, they would recognize it as your blessing on their life. Let them always look to you for honor instead of chasing after the recognition of men. Let their heart's desire be to please you alone.

MARCH 4

"O God, you are my God; I earnestly search for you."

PSALM 63:1 (NLT)

I pray each of my children would call you their God. I pray each one would earnestly search for you on a daily basis. Thank you that your word promises when they seek you with all their heart, they will find you. Let each one find you.

MARCH 5

"Their own tongues will ruin them,"

PSALM 64:8 (NLT)

I pray each of my children would recognize the power of their words. I pray that they would learn this truth early in life. I pray that they would daily choose to use their words to praise and honor you, and to love and encourage others. Protect them from ruin by their own tongues. Thank you.

MARCH 6

"You faithfully answer our prayers with awesome deeds, O God our savior."

PSALM 65:5 (NLT)

Thank you for your faithfulness toward each of my children. Thank you that you never fail to hear their prayers and you faithfully answer, not just with good deeds, but with awesome deeds! I pray my children would see your glory and they would recognize your hand at work in response to their prayers. Raise them up to be mighty prayer warriors. Let them be known as people of prayer.

MARCH 7

"Come and see what our God has done, what awesome miracles he performs for people!"

PSALM 66:5 (NLT)

I pray each of my children would come to you; and as they do, I ask you to open their eyes to see what you have done, what you are doing, and what you will do. I pray they would see your miracles in their lives and in the lives of the people they pray for. I pray others would come and see Jesus in each of them.

MARCH 8

"May God be merciful and bless us. May his face smile with favor on us."

PSALM 67:1 (NLT)

Lord, please be merciful and bless each of my children. I pray your face would smile with favor upon each one of them on a daily basis.

MARCH 9

"Praise the Lord; praise God our savior! For each day he carries us in his arms."

PSALM 68:19 (NLT)

I thank you and praise you that each day you carry my children in your arms. Thank you for the peace and joy that gives me as their parent. I pray they would be aware of your arms around them, they would experience your strength and peace, and they would praise you daily.

MARCH 10

"Passion for your house has consumed me."

PSALM 69:9 (NLT)

I pray each of my children would be consumed by passion for your house. Let that passion be the guiding force in their lives. Consume each one with you.

MARCH 11

"But may all who search for you be filled with joy and gladness in you."

PSALM 70:4 (NLT)

I pray each of my children would search for you daily. Please draw them to yourself. As they search for you, please fill them with gladness and joy. Let them see that gladness and joy ultimately come from you.

MARCH 12

"My life is an example to many, because you have been my strength and protection."

PSALM 71:7 (NLT)

I pray each of my children would be an example to many. Please let each of their lives exemplify your love, mercy, generosity, and peace. I pray their example would lead many others to Christ. Thank you that you are their strength and protection. I pray those who know them and come in contact with them would see that you are, and have been, their strength and protection.

MARCH 13

"May they fear you as long as the sun shines, as long as the moon remains in the sky. Yes, forever!"

PSALM 72:5 (NLT)

May each of my children fear you as long as the suns shines, as long as the moon remains in the sky. Yes, forever! I pray they would honor, revere, and obey you on a daily basis.

MARCH 14

"You guide me with your counsel, leading me to a glorious destiny."

PSALM 73:24 (NLT)

Thank you for the glorious destiny planned for each of my children. Please guide each of them with your counsel. I pray you would give each of them the discernment to see and hear your counsel, and the wisdom to follow it.

MARCH 15

You, O God, are my king from ages past, bringing salvation to the earth.

PSALM 74:12 (NLT)

I praise you because you are the King and Savior of my children. Thank you that you have set them free. I pray each one would live with the knowledge of you as King and Savior. Please use my children to proclaim your salvation to the earth.

MARCH 16

"We give thanks because you are near."

PSALM 75:1 (NLT)

Thank you, Lord, that you are always near to each of my children, and that you will remain near to them every second of their life. I pray each one would recognize your nearness in good moments and bad; and they would give you thanks.

MARCH 17

"...he has broken the fiery arrows of the enemy, the shields and swords and weapons of war."

PSALM 76:3 (NLT)

Thank you, Lord, that no enemy can lift a hand in victory against my children because you are the one who protects them. Please destroy any plans, arrows, shields, swords or weapons of war that the enemy would try to use against any of my children today and every day of their lives.

MARCH 18

"I cannot stop thinking about your mighty works."

PSALM 77:12 (NLT)

I pray each of my children would not be able to stop thinking about your mighty works. I pray their first thought every day would be of you; and their last thought before falling asleep would be of you. Open their eyes to see the mighty things you are doing in their lives and in the world. Thank you!

MARCH 19

"So each generation should set its hope anew on God, not forgetting his glorious miracles and obeying his commands."

PSALM 78:7 (NLT)

I pray my children's generation would set its hope anew on you, that they wouldn't forget your glorious miracles, and that they would obey your commands. I pray my children would lead the way among their generation.

MARCH 20

"Do not hold us guilty for the sins of our ancestors!"

PSALM 79:8 (NLT)

Please do not hold my children guilty of the sins of their ancestors. Please break any strongholds that may have come through their history. Heal any broken places. Destroy any generational sins in their lives. Break any chains that bind them, and let the power and hold of any sins of their ancestors end with them.

MARCH 21

"Turn us again to yourself, O God. Make your face shine down upon us. Only then will we be saved."

PSALM 80:3 (NLT)

I pray each of my children would turn again to you today. I pray your face would shine down upon each one of them. Thank you that you save them. Thank you that you remain faithful to complete the work you started in each of them.

MARCH 22

"But no, my people wouldn't listen. Israel did not want me around. So I let them follow their own stubborn desires, living according to their own ideas."

PSALM 81:11-12 (NLT)

I pray each of my children would listen to you and wouldn't follow their own stubborn desires. I pray they wouldn't live according to their own ideas, but according to your Word. I pray any time they stop listening to you, that you would lovingly draw them back.

MARCH 23

"Give justice to the poor and the orphan; uphold the rights of the oppressed and the destitute."

PSALM 82:3 (NLT)

I pray each of my children would see the poor, the orphan, the oppressed, and the destitute with your eyes. I pray their hearts would be to help give justice to the least of these in our world.

MARCH 24

"O God, do not be silent! Do not be deaf. Do not be quiet, O God."

PSALM 83:1 (NLT)

I pray you would not be silent in the life of my children. Speak into their lives. Let them hear your voice. I pray you would not be deaf to them. Hear the cry of their hearts, even when they aren't able to express it to you. Do not be quiet where they are concerned.

MARCH 25

"I long, yes, I faint with longing to enter the courts of the Lord. With my whole being, body and soul, I will shout joyfully to the living God."

PSALM 84:2 (NLT)

I pray each of my children would come to a place in their lives where they faint with longing for you and your presence. I pray they would shout joyfully to you with their whole being, body and soul.

MARCH 26

"Righteousness goes as a herald before him, preparing the way for his steps."

PSALM 85:13 (NLT)

Just as righteousness goes before you, Lord, I pray righteousness would go before each of my children. Please prepare the way for their steps and let them walk in that way. Let each one of my children be known for their righteousness.

MARCH 27

"Teach me your ways, O Lord, that I may live according to your truth! Grant me purity of heart, so that I may honor you."

PSALM 86:11 (NLT)

Please teach each of my children your ways so they may live according to your truth. Please cleanse them and create pure hearts in them. Let them honor you every day of their lives.

MARCH 28

"I will count Egypt and Babylon among those who know me"

PSALM 87:4 (NLT)

Lord, I pray each of my children would be counted among those who know you. I pray you would draw them deeper and closer to you on a daily basis. Give them wisdom and insight into your character, your word, and your will. Place in each of their hearts a deep longing to know you that motivates them to seek you and develop a relationship with you.

MARCH 29

"O Lord, God of my salvation, I cry out to you by day. I come to you at night."

PSALM 88:1 (NLT)

I pray each of my children would recognize that you are the God of their salvation. I pray they would humble themselves and cry out to you by day. I pray that they would come to you every night. I pray they would know they could cry out and come to you at any time and find you there.

MARCH 30

"You are their glorious strength. It pleases you to make us strong."

PSALM 89:17 (NLT)

Thank you, Lord, that you are the glorious strength of my children. Thank you that it pleases you to make each of them strong. Please help them learn to rely on you for strength and not on themselves or anyone or anything else.

MARCH 31

"Teach us to realize the brevity of life, so that we may grow in wisdom."

PSALM 90:12 (NLT)

Lord I pray each of my children will realize the brevity of life. I pray they would live every moment to the full. I pray they would recognize each moment and each day are sacred gifts from you. Let them use the time they have to bring honor and glory to your great name.

APRIL 1

"His faithful promises are your armor and protection."

PSALM 91:4 (NLT)

Thank you that your faithful promises were given for each of my children. Thank you that those promises will be their armor and protection. Please teach them to stand on your promises and find strength in that place.

APRIL 2

"For they are transplanted to the Lord's own house. They flourish in the courts of our God."

PSALM 92:13 (NLT)

Thank you that you have transplanted my children to your own house. I pray they would flourish in your courts, grow strong and produce fruit that will last.

APRIL 3

"The world stands firm and cannot be shaken."

PSALM 93:1 (NLT)

Thank you that the world stands firm and cannot be shaken because you are God and you reign over it all. I pray on the days things seem to be falling apart that my children would recognize you are holding everything together. Help each one to stand firm in you.

APRIL 4

"When doubts filled my mind, your comfort gave me renewed hope and cheer."

PSALM 94:19 (NLT)

I pray when doubts fill the minds of my children that your comfort would renew their hope and cheer them on. When they doubt themselves, I pray you would encourage them with your truth. When they doubt you, I pray they would bring those doubts to you. I ask you to strengthen them to cling to you when doubts can't be answered. Teach them and help them to rely on faith.

APRIL 5

"Come let us worship and bow down. Let us kneel before the Lord our maker, for he is our God."

PSALM 95:6-7 (NLT)

I pray each of my children would worship you today. I pray they would humble themselves, kneel before you and recognize you are Lord, you are our maker, and you are the God of the universe. Teach them to live in that place of humility and recognition of your Lordship daily.

APRIL 6

"Each day proclaim the good news that he saves."

PSALM 96:2 (NLT)

I pray each day my children would proclaim the good news that Jesus saves, by their words, their actions, their expressions, and their attitudes. Let the world see Jesus when they see my children.

APRIL 7

"He protects the lives of his godly people and rescues them from the power of the wicked."

PSALM 97:10 (NLT)

Thank you that you protect the lives of each of my children. I pray as they proclaim your good news daily that you would rescue them from any power of the wicked, and from every scheme or trap of the enemy.

APRIL 8

"Make a joyful symphony before the Lord, the King!"

PSALM 98:6 (NLT)

Thank you that my children are part of your symphony. I pray each one would play their part. I pray each of my children would be and do all you designed and created them for in this life, and by so doing bring praise and honor to you.

APRIL 9

"You have acted with justice and righteousness..."

PSALM 99:4 (NLT)

I pray each of my children would act with justice and righteousness all the days of their lives. I pray they would be an accurate reflection of you.

APRIL 10

"For the Lord is good. His unfailing love continues forever, and his faithfulness continues to each generation."

PSALM 100:5 (NLT)

Thank you that your faithfulness extends to the generation of my children. Thank you that your love continues forever. Thank you that you've never failed, and you won't fail my children. I pray each of my children would acknowledge that you are God and you are good.

APRIL 11

"I will search for faithful people to be my companions."

PSALM 101:6 (NLT)

I pray that each of my children would search for and find faithful people to be their companions who will walk through life with them – friends who will encourage and challenge them in their faith; and always point them to Jesus.

APRIL 12

"Bend down to listen and answer me quickly when I call to you."

PSALM 102:2 (NLT)

Thank you that you always bend down to listen to my children. Thank you that you hear their cries and longings; and you know the desires of their hearts. Thank you that you know them better than they know themselves. Please answer them quickly when they call to you. Let them know the reality of your faithfulness and love.

APRIL 13

"Let all that I am praise the Lord"

PSALM 103:1 (NLT)

I pray each of my children will daily praise you with all that they are. I pray they come to understand they can choose to praise you no matter the circumstances of their lives. I pray they would daily make the choice to recognize and praise you as Lord.

APRIL 14

"The Lord takes pleasure in all he has made!"

PSALM 104:31 (NLT)

I pray you would always take pleasure in my children. May each of their lives bring honor and glory to your name. May their obedience, sacrifice and praise daily bring you pleasure.

APRIL 15

"Search for the Lord and for his strength; continually seek him."

PSALM 105:4 (NLT)

I pray each of my children would search for you and your strength today. I pray each one would continually seek you. I pray they wouldn't let any person or circumstance or experience keep them from seeking you and your strength.

APRIL 16

"Again and again He rescued them…"

PSALM 106:43 (NLT)

Thank you that you are the one who rescues my children. Thank you that you never give up on them. I pray you would rescue them again and again, every time they need rescue.

APRIL 17

"Those who are wise will take all this to heart; they will see in our history the faithful love of the Lord."

PSALM 107:43 (NLT)

I pray you would open the eyes of my children to see in our history your faithful love, and that they would take it to heart. I pray this knowledge would transform each of their lives.

APRIL 18

"My heart is confident in you, O God…"

PSALM 108:1 (NLT)

I pray the hearts of each of my children would always be confident in you. I pray, with your help, they will do mighty things and defeat any plans of the enemy.

APRIL 19

**"But deal well with me, O Sovereign Lord, for the sake
of your own reputation."**

PSALM 109:21 (NLT)

For the sake of your reputation, Lord; please deal well with each of my children. Do whatever it takes in each of their lives so that they bring honor and glory to your great name.

APRIL 20

"The Lord stands at your right hand to protect you."

PSALM 110:5 (NLT)

Thank you that you always stand ready to protect each of my children. Thank you that you never look away and you always have your eye on each of them. I trust you to protect them.

APRIL 21

**"Fear of the Lord is the foundation of true wisdom. All
who obey his commands will grow in wisdom."**

PSALM 111:10 (NLT)

I pray each of my children would develop respect for you as God. I pray they would build their lives on that foundation. Thank you that as they obey your commands you promise to grow them in wisdom. I pray they would be known for godly wisdom.

APRIL 22

"Light shines in the darkness for the godly. They are generous, compassionate, and righteous."

PSALM 112:4 (NLT)

Thank you for sending your light into our dark world. Thank you that your light shines in the darkness for my children. I pray your light would always illuminate the way for each of them, especially in those moments and places when darkness seems to close in. I pray that they would shine like you do, and they would be generous, compassionate, and righteous.

APRIL 23

"Who can compare with the Lord, our God, who is enthroned on high?"

PSALM 113:5 (NLT)

I pray every time my children compare any thing, any person, any thought, any idea, or any philosophy with you that they will see that nothing can compare with you. I pray they recognize that you are the one true God, enthroned on high, and worship you.

APRIL 24

**"The Red Sea saw them coming and hurried out of
their way."**

PSALM 114:3 (NLT)

I pray you would work the same way in the lives of each of my children. Please clear the way before them and lead them. Let them see your miracles as they go.

APRIL 25

**"May you be blessed by the Lord, who made heaven
and earth."**

PSALM 115:15 (NLT)

Please richly bless each of my children from your glorious riches. Bless them in whatever way you know is best for them. Thank you for the way you have blessed me by choosing me to be their parent.

APRIL 26

**"He has saved me from death, my eyes from tears, my
feet from stumbling."**

PSALM 116:8 (NLT)

I ask you to save each of my children from death, physically and spiritually. Please save their eyes from tears, and save their feet from stumbling. Help them to walk in your presence daily.

APRIL 27

"For his unfailing love for us is powerful, the Lord's faithfulness endures forever."

PSALM 117:2 (NLT)

Thank you for the unfailing love you have for each of my children. Thank you that your powerful love transforms their lives. Thank you that your love for them will endure forever. Thank you that there is nothing they could ever do that would make you stop loving them.

APRIL 28

"It is better to take refuge in the Lord than to trust in people."

PSALM 118:8 (NLT)

I pray each of my children would take refuge in you. I pray they would trust in your word more than they trust in people. I pray they would trust in your wisdom and not in the wisdom of the world. I pray they would take refuge in you when people betray them or let them down. Thank you for being their refuge.

APRIL 29

**"They do not compromise with evil, and they walk only
in his paths."**

PSALM 119:3 (NLT)

I pray each of my children would not compromise with evil, no matter the attraction and no matter the cost. I pray each one would walk only in your paths all the days of their lives.

APRIL 30

**"Rescue me, O Lord, from liars and from all
deceitful people."**

PSALM 120:3 (NLT)

Please rescue my children from liars and from all deceitful people. Please keep them from falling into the habit of lying and the sin of deceitfulness. Let them be known for honesty and integrity. I pray each of my children would cry out to you today. I am grateful that as they do, you hear their cries and answer them.

MAY 1

"The Lord keeps you from all harm and watches over your life."

PSALM 121:7 (NLT)

Thank you for watching over the life of each of my children. Thank you that you never sleep, you never close your eyes, you never look away. Thank you that they are always in your sight. Please keep them from stumbling, be their protection, and keep them from all harm.

MAY 2

"We keep looking to the Lord our God for his mercy…"

PSALM 123:2 (NLT)

I pray each of my children would look to you for your mercy, and that they would keep looking to you for your mercy. Help them to see that without your mercy they are lost. Thank you that you always deal with us with your great mercy.

MAY 3

"What if the Lord had not been on our side?"

PSALM 124:1 (NLT)

Thank you that my children will never know life without you by their side. Thank you that you are the one who stands guard over each of them. Thank you for being their shield and defender, their strength and comfort.

May 4

**"O Lord, do good to those who are good, whose hearts
are in tune with you."**

Psalm 125:4 (NLT)

I pray the hearts of each of my children would be in tune with you every day
of their lives. Thank you that your heart is to do good to them. Open their
eyes to recognize your goodness in their lives.

May 5

"When the Lord brought back…"

Psalm 126:1 (NLT)

Thank you that you are the God of second chances. I pray whenever any
of my children gets away from you that you would gently bring them back.
Thank you for your patience and faithfulness toward each of them. Thank
you for pursuing them and for bringing them back again.

May 6

"…for God gives rest to his loved ones."

Psalm 127:2 (NLT)

Thank you, Lord, that you give rest to my children. In those moments when
things are stressful or overwhelming I pray they would turn to you and find
rest.

MAY 7

"You will enjoy the fruit of your labor."

PSALM 128:2 (NLT)

I pray my children would enjoy the fruit of their labor. Please use their gifts, talents, and experiences for your kingdom and glory.

MAY 8

"...he has cut me free from the ropes of the ungodly."

PSALM 129:4 (NLT)

I pray you would cut each of my children free from the ropes of the ungodly, and free from the snares of the enemy. Thank you for the freedom you provide for them in Christ. Please teach them to live in that freedom.

MAY 9

"I long for the Lord..."

PSALM 130:6 (NLT)

Please put a longing for you in the hearts of each of my children. Help them discover that even a moment without you is a wasted moment. Call to their hearts each morning as they wake up. Let your call be so strong on their lives they can't turn away.

MAY 10

"Lord, my heart is not proud; my eyes are not haughty."

PSALM 131:1 (NLT)

I pray you would protect my children from the sin of pride. Break down any strongholds of pride in their lives. Point it out to them and help them choose to humble themselves before you. Let them choose humility in every relationship.

MAY 11

"...my anointed one will be a light for my people."

PSALM 132:17 (NLT)

I pray each of my children would be a light for your people. I pray they would think your thoughts, speak your words, and do your will. Let others see Jesus in each of them.

MAY 12

"How wonderful and pleasant it is when brothers live together in harmony!"

PSALM 133:1 (NLT)

I pray my children would always live together in harmony. I pray they would always choose forgiveness, honesty, and love in their relationships with one another. I pray when we, their parents, are gone, they would continue in that harmony.

MAY 13

**"Lift your hands toward the sanctuary, and praise
the Lord."**

PSALM 134:2 (NLT)

I pray each of my children would lift their hands and praise you consistently.
Please remove anything in their lives that would distract them from praising
you. Convict them of the sin of idolatry any time they choose to put something else in your place in their lives.

MAY 14

"I know the greatness of the Lord..."

PSALM 135:5 (NLT)

I pray each of my children would experience and know your greatness in their
lives.

MAY 15

**"Give thanks to the Lord, for he is good! His faithful
love endures forever."**

PSALM 136:1 (NLT)

Thank you that your faithful love for my children will last through every day
of their lives. Thank you for your goodness toward them. Please let them
understand how much you love them.

MAY 16

"But how can we sing the songs of the Lord while in a pagan land?"

PSALM 137:4 (NLT)

I pray even in the midst of our world and culture that my children would be able to sing your praises. Help them to see your goodness and faithfulness in spite of dark times and difficult days. Please put a song in their hearts.

MAY 17

"The Lord will work out his plans for my life..."

PSALM 138:8 (NLT)

Thank you that you are and you will work out your plans for the life of each of my children! Thank you that even when they don't know which direction to go, you do. Thank you that you hold the future, and you will direct them. They have nothing to fear. Teach them to rest in you.

MAY 18

"Point out anything in me that offends you, and lead me along the path of everlasting life."

PSALM 139:24 (NLT)

Please point out anything that offends you in the lives of my children. Open their hearts to hear your spirit. Strengthen and encourage them to change or remove those offensive things from their lives. Let them choose to follow you on the path of everlasting life no matter the cost.

MAY 19

"O Lord, rescue me from evil people. Protect me from those who are violent…"

PSALM 140:1 (NLT)

Please rescue my children from evil people. Protect each of them from those who are violent. Don't let them be victims of abuse. I ask you to rescue and protect them from these things every day of their lives.

MAY 20

"Take control of what I say, O Lord, and guard my lips."

PSALM 141:3 (NLT)

I pray you would guard the lips of each of my children. Take control of what they say. Teach them to take every thought and every word captive to Christ. Let them use their words to bring encouragement and life.

May 21

"When I am overwhelmed, you alone know the way I should turn."

Psalm 142:3 (NLT)

I pray whenever my children feel overwhelmed they would look to you. Please direct them during those times when circumstances overwhelm. Thank you that nothing overwhelms you. Thank you that you know the way they should turn every time.

May 22

"I thirst for you as parched land thirsts for rain."

Psalm 143:6 (NLT)

I pray my children would thirst for you as parched land thirsts for rain. Please create that thirst in each of them. Help them to see their deep need to spend time with you daily. Let them learn that you are the only one who can fulfill their needs and the longings of their hearts.

MAY 23

"May our sons flourish in their youth like well-nurtured plants. May our daughters be like graceful pillars, carved to beautify a palace."

PSALM 144:12 (NLT)

I pray each of my children would flourish in their youth. Please bring people into their lives who will nurture their faith. Please raise them up in strength. Let your beauty shine through them.

MAY 24

"When you open your hand you satisfy the hunger and thirst of every living thing."

PSALM 145:16 (NLT)

Thank you that you are the source of everything my children need. Thank you that you open your hand to satisfy their hunger and thirst. Thank you that there is no need you can't meet. Thank you that you open your hand toward them as soon as they ask. Thank you that you provide for them out of your glorious riches.

MAY 25

"Don't put your confidence in powerful people; there is no help for you there."

PSALM 146:3 (NLT)

I pray my children would not put their confidence in powerful people. I pray each one would realize their help comes from you. Let them daily put their trust, hope, and confidence in you.

MAY 26

"He heals the brokenhearted and bandages their wounds."

PSALM 147:3 (NLT)

Thank you that you always heal the brokenhearted and you bandage their wounds. I pray any time my children are wounded or broken hearted that they bring their pain to you. Help me trust you to comfort, strengthen, and heal them.

MAY 27

"He has made his people strong..."

PSALM 148:14 (NLT)

Please make my children strong in you. Give them everything they need to face the challenges that come into their daily lives. Teach them about your strength. Remind them that you are the source of their strength. Help them look to you and trust in your ability and power in their lives.

MAY 28

"...he crowns the humble with victory."

PSALM149:4 (NLT)

I pray each of my children would daily choose to humble themselves. Please teach them to choose humility. Let them be an accurate reflection of you. Thank you for the victory promised to them as they choose humility.

MAY 29

"Praise him for his mighty works; praise his unequaled greatness!"

PSALM 150:2 (NLT)

I pray each of my children would see your mighty works in their lives, that they would see your unequaled greatness, and that it would lead them to praise you.

MAY 30

"My child, if sinners entice you, turn your back on them!"

PROVERBS 1:10 (NLT)

I pray any time sin or sinners entice my children they would turn their back on it. Open their eyes to see sin. Convict them of the truth that sin always leads to death. Empower them to choose righteousness no matter the cost. Let them be known as people who stand up for righteousness in their family, community, and world.

MAY 31

**"Tune your ears to wisdom, and concentrate on
understanding."**

PROVERBS 2:2 (NLT)

I pray each of my children would daily tune their ears to wisdom. I pray in every relationship, interaction, and decision they would concentrate on understanding. Thank you for being the source of wisdom and understanding for my children. Let them tap into that source.

JUNE 1

**"Never let loyalty and kindness leave you! Tie them
around your neck as a reminder. Write them deep within your heart."**

PROVERBS 3:3 (NLT)

I pray each of my children would have loyalty and kindness written deep within heir hearts. Let their loyalty to you result in kindness to others. When they forget, please remind them.

JUNE 2

"Get wisdom; develop good judgment."

PROVERBS 4:5 (NLT)

Please give wisdom to each of my children. Let them see things from your perspective. Please develop good judgment in them, even from an early age. Thank you!

JUNE 3

"He will die for lack of self-control…"

PROVERBS 5:23 (NLT)

Please develop the power of self-control in each of my children. Teach them the value of self-control. Let them see the positive results of self-control in their daily lives. Give them the wisdom and strength to make difficult choices of self-control. Please teach them this habit early in life.

JUNE 4

"My son, obey your father's commands, and don't neglect your mother's instruction."

PROVERBS 6:20 (NLT)

I pray each of my children would remember the things their parents have taught them. Teach them the value of obedience and submission to authority. Remove any spirit of rebellion in them.

JUNE 5

"He was like a bird flying into a snare, little knowing it would cost him his life."

PROVERBS 7:23 (NLT)

I pray you would protect each of my children from the snares of the enemy. Help them to see these traps and choose to follow after you. Teach them the truth that sin always leads to death; and give them insight, wisdom, and strength to choose life.

JUNE 6

"All who fear the Lord will hate evil."

PROVERBS 8:13 (NLT)

I pray each of my children would daily live and walk in the fear of the Lord. I pray they would hate evil as you do.

JUNE 7

"...Knowledge of the Holy One results in good judgment."

PROVERBS 9:10 (NLT)

I pray each of my children would have such intimate knowledge of you that the result would be good judgment in their lives. Give them good judgment in each daily decision whether large or small. Let them be known as people of good judgment.

JUNE 8

**"The lips of the godly speak helpful words, but the
mouth of the wicked speaks perverse words."**

PROVERBS 10:32 (NLT)

I pray each of my children would recognize the power of their words. I pray they would daily choose to use their words to give life. I pray they would speak helpful words that bring encouragement, hope, truth, and love. Help them choose not to speak words that are seen as perverse, or words that discourage, harm, or bring death.

JUNE 9

**"The generous will prosper; those who refresh others
will themselves be refreshed."**

PROVERBS 11:25 (NLT)

I pray you would teach each of my children to be generous in every area of their lives – generous with their finances, their time, their talents, with forgiveness, and patience. May they be generous of spirit. I pray they would daily refresh others with their generosity. Thank you that as they do, you will refresh them.

JUNE 10

"Work hard and become a leader..."

PROVERBS 12:24 (NLT)

I pray each of my children would work hard at whatever you give them to do. I pray you would raise them up to be leaders in their families, communities, churches, and jobs. Teach them that leadership comes through service.

JUNE 11

"Pride leads to conflict; those who take advice are wise."

PROVERBS 13:10 (NLT)

I pray each of my children would learn early that pride leads to conflict. I pray they would daily choose to humble themselves. Whenever they experience conflict, remind them to look for pride and to change their attitude. I pray you would bring people in their life who will give them godly advice, and that they would see the value of that advice.

JUNE 12

"...blessed are those who help the poor."

PROVERBS 14:21 (NLT)

I pray you would give each of my children a heart for the poor. Open their eyes to see the poor as you do. Open their hearts to love them like you do. And give them your wisdom to know best how to help them. May they be known as followers of Christ because of the love they have for the poor.

JUNE 13

"A gentle answer deflects anger..."

PROVERBS 15:1 (NLT)

I pray each of my children would learn the truth of this verse early. Hide it in their hearts and when arguments arise, show them the power of a gentle answer.

JUNE 14

"Better to be patient than powerful..."

PROVERBS 16:32 (NLT)

I pray you would teach each of my children to be patient. Give them wisdom and strength to wait on you. Teach them to exercise patience in their relationships and in their jobs. Give them patience to wait on their dreams. Thank you!

JUNE 15

"Love prospers when a fault is forgiven, but dwelling on it separates close friends."

PROVERBS 17:9 (NLT)

I pray each of my children would daily practice forgiveness in their relationships. Develop in each of them a forgiving spirit that doesn't dwell on wrongs suffered, quickly offers forgiveness, always looks for the good, and chooses to assume the best about others. Make them forgivers like you.

JUNE 16

"Unfriendly people care only about themselves."

PROVERBS 18:1 (NLT)

I pray each of my children would have open spirits toward the people you bring into their lives. Teach them to choose and offer friendliness. Let them demonstrate your love through their friendliness.

JUNE 17

"To acquire wisdom is to love yourself..."

PROVERBS 19:8 (NLT)

I pray each of my children would daily seek wisdom. I pray they would ask you for wisdom. Thank you that you promise to generously give them wisdom when they ask you for it. Help them to see life through your perspective.

JUNE 18

"Ears to hear and eyes to see — both are gifts from the Lord."

PROVERBS 20:12 (NLT)

Thank you for the physical ears and eyes of my children; but even more than that, I pray you would give them spiritual ears and eyes. Help each one to hear and see below the surface. Help them to hear with your ears and to see with your eyes

JUNE 19

"The Lord is more pleased when we do what is right and just than when we offer him sacrifices."

PROVERBS 21:3 (NLT)

I pray each of my children would daily choose to do what is right and just. Give them your divine wisdom to see those things and the courage to choose to act.

JUNE 20

"Choose a good reputation over great riches; being held in high esteem is better than silver or gold."

PROVERBS 22:1 (NLT)

I pray each of my children would know the value of a good reputation and that they would choose a good reputation over great riches. I pray each one would be held in high esteem by those who know them and know of them.

JUNE 21

"O my son, give me your heart. May your eyes take delight in following my ways."

PROVERBS 23:26 (NLT)

I pray each of my children would daily give their hearts to you. I pray their eyes would take delight in following your ways. As they do, let them experience your pleasure and see your glory.

JUNE 22

"An honest answer is like a kiss of friendship."

PROVERBS 24:26 (NLT)

Please develop in each of my children the character trait of honesty. Help them to always tell the truth in love and to always give an honest answer. Develop in them the spirit of authenticity.

JUNE 23

"A person without self-control is like a city with broken-down walls."

PROVERBS 25:28 (NLT)

Please develop the habit of self-control in each of my children. Let their self-control serve as protection for them from the schemes of the enemy, just as a fortified city is protected by its walls.

JUNE 24

"A quarrelsome person starts fights..."

PROVERBS 26:21 (NLT)

I pray each of my children would develop the practice of honest encouraging conversation and that they would not be quarrelsome. I pray they would not be those who start fights but those who bring peace to every conversation and every situation.

JUNE 25

"Never abandon a friend— either yours or your father's."

PROVERBS 27:10 (NLT)

I pray my children will each be faithful friends. I pray they will be known for their loyalty, and that they will never abandon a friend.

JUNE 26

"...the godly are as bold as lions."

PROVERBS 28:1 (NLT)

I pray each of my children would be as bold as lions. I pray they would live bold lives for you and your Kingdom. I pray you would develop in each of them courage, self-confidence, and faith.

JUNE 27

"An angry person starts fights; a hot-tempered person commits all kinds of sin."

PROVERBS 29:22 (NLT)

I pray each of my children would learn early in life how to deal with anger. I pray they would not be hot-tempered and they would not start fights. I pray they would learn to think before they speak and to weigh their words carefully.

JUNE 28

"Every word of God proves true."

PROVERBS 30:5 (NLT)

I pray in the lives of each of my children your word will prove to be true. Let them see and remember the truth of your every word. Teach them to base their lives on that truth.

JUNE 29

"She is clothed with strength and dignity, and she laughs without fear of the future."

PROVERBS 31:25 (NLT)

I pray each of my children will be clothed with strength and dignity. I pray they will be filled with peace and joy. I pray the peace found in their relationship with you will lead to a life without fear of the future.

JUNE 30

"If pleasing people were my goal, I would not be Christ's servant."

GALATIANS 1:10 (NLT)

I pray each of my children would live their lives not to please people, but to please you. Let their lives be free of the fear of what people think about them.

JULY 1

"I do not treat the grace of God as meaningless."

GALATIANS 2:21 (NLT)

I pray my children would never treat your grace as meaningless. Let them daily live in the freedom found in your grace. Let their lives show the world the power of your grace.

JULY 2

"For the meaning of Jesus Christ's death was made as clear to you as if you had seen a picture of his death on the cross."

GALATIANS 3:1 (NLT)

I pray the meaning of Jesus' death would always remain clear to my children. I pray they would live in the freedom found through their faith in Christ; and that this freedom would transform their lives.

JULY 3

"God sent him to buy freedom for us who were slaves to the law, so that he could adopt us as his very own children."

GALATIANS 4:5 (NLT)

I pray each of my children would always look to you as their father. I pray they would understand that you have the heart of a father toward them and that they would call out to you as their daddy. Thank you that you have made them your children.

JULY 4

"I am trusting the Lord to keep you from believing false teachings."

GALATIANS 5:10 (NLT)

Please keep each of my children from believing false teachings. Please guide them to churches where truth is taught and practiced. Protect them from people who would influence them with false teachings. Surround them with those who lead them to truth.

JULY 5

"For we are each responsible for our own conduct."

GALATIANS 6:5 (NLT)

I pray each of my children would take responsibility for their own conduct. I pray they would not assign blame to other people or circumstances for their behavior; but that they would learn early in life the power they have to choose their actions, attitudes, and words.

JULY 6

"...because we are united with Christ..."

EPHESIANS 1:11 (NLT)

Thank you that each of my children have been united with Christ. Please teach them to live in the reality of that truth. Draw each of them deeper and closer to you.

JULY 7

"For we are God's masterpiece. He has created us anew in Christ Jesus, so we can do the good things he planned for us long ago."

EPHESIANS 2:10 (NLT)

Thank you for the masterpiece you designed each of my children to be. Thank you for the good things you have planned for them to do. Thank you that you created each of my children anew in Jesus.

July 8

"By God's grace and mighty power, I have been given the privilege of serving him by spreading this Good News."

EPHESIANS 3:7 (NLT)

Thank you for giving each of my children the privilege of serving you and spreading your Good News. I pray they would each recognize this privilege. Thank you for the grace and power you have given to them to spread your Good News. Thank you for the ways you are going to use them for your Kingdom.

July 9

"Always be humble and gentle. Be patient with each other, making allowance for each other's faults because of your love."

EPHESIANS 4:2 (NLT)

I pray each of my children would be humble, gentle, and patient. I pray they would remember we are all learning and growing, and that they would make allowance for each other's faults. I pray they would love others unconditionally.

JULY 10

"Imitate God, therefore, in everything you do, because you are his dear children."

EPHESIANS 5:1 (NLT)

I pray each of my children would imitate you in everything they do. Thank you for making them your children. Let them be an accurate reflection of you.

JULY 11

"Pray in the Spirit at all times and on every occasion. Stay alert and be persistent in your prayers for all believers everywhere."

EPHESIANS 6:18 (NLT)

Please teach each of my children to pray in the Spirit at all times and on every occasion. I pray that in every circumstance their first instinct would be to pray. Please teach them to be persistent in prayer, never giving up hope.

JULY 12

"And I trust that my life will bring honor to Christ, whether I live or die."

PHILIPPIANS 1:20 (NLT)

I pray the lives of each of my children would bring honor to you, in their living and in their dying.

JULY 13

"Don't be selfish; don't try to impress others. Be humble, thinking of others as better than yourselves."

PHILIPPIANS 2:3 (NLT)

Please develop in each of my children an attitude of selflessness. Teach them to live only to please you and not to impress others. Help them to daily humble themselves and to think of others first.

JULY 14

"Whatever happens, my dear brothers and sisters, rejoice in the Lord."

PHILIPPIANS 3:1 (NLT)

I pray each of my children would learn that no matter what happens in their life they can rejoice in you. Let them know you so well that they are able to trust you and to rejoice always.

JULY 15

"Fix your thoughts on what is true, and honorable, and right, and pure, and lovely, and admirable. Think about things that are excellent and worthy of praise."

PHILIPPIANS 4:8 (NLT)

I pray each of my children would learn to take their thoughts captive to Christ. I pray they would daily think on what is true, honorable, right, pure, lovely, admirable, excellent, and worthy of praise.

JULY 16

"For we have heard of your faith in Christ Jesus and your love for all of God's people,"

COLOSSIANS 1:4 (NLT)

I pray each of my children would be known for their faith in Christ Jesus and their love for all of God's people.

JULY 17

"Let your roots grow down into him, and let your lives be built on him."

COLOSSIANS 2:7 (NLT)

Please strengthen and grow the spiritual roots of each of my children. Let their roots grow down deep into you. I pray each one would build their life on you.

July 18

"...set your sights on the realities of heaven..."

Colossians 3:1 (NLT)

I pray each of my children would live with their sights set on the reality of heaven. Let them make eternal investments and live for eternal purposes.

July 19

"Live wisely among those who are not believers, and make the most of every opportunity."

Colossians 4:5 (NLT)

I pray each of my children would live wisely among those who are not believers. I pray Christ would be evident in their lives. I pray they would make the most of every opportunity they have to live what they believe.

July 20

"Christ made us right with God; he made us pure and holy, and he freed us from sin."

1 Corinthians 1:30 (NLT)

Thank you for making each of my children right with you. Thank you for making them pure and holy; and for freeing them from sin. Please continue the work you started in each of their lives. Help each one to live in the knowledge of this reality.

JULY 21

"...for we have the mind of Christ."

1 CORINTHIANS 2:16 (NLT)

Thank you that you have given each of my children the mind of Christ. Let them think your thoughts, speak your words, have your attitude, and do your will.

JULY 22

"Stop deceiving yourselves."

1 CORINTHIANS 3:18 (NLT)

I pray my children would not deceive themselves. I pray they would not think they are wise by the world's standards but that they would base their lives on your wisdom and truth.

JULY 23

"For the Kingdom of God is not just a lot of talk; it is living by God's power."

1 CORINTHIANS 4:20 (NLT)

I pray each of my children would daily live in your power. I pray they would live with the knowledge that your kingdom is not just a lot of talk, but that it will be reflected in their actions.

JULY 24

"Christ, our Passover Lamb, has been sacrificed for us."

1 CORINTHIANS 5:7 (NLT)

Thank you for the sacrifice you made for each of my children. I pray they would live each day in light of that sacrifice; and that they would lay down their lives for you just as you have for them.

JULY 25

"So you must honor God with your body."

1 CORINTHIANS 6:20 (NLT)

I pray each of my children would daily honor God with their bodies. Please protect them from sexual immorality. Protect them from any type of eating disorder. Teach them to discipline and train their physical bodies, not for worldly purposes, but to bring honor to you.

JULY 26

"For the believing wife brings holiness to her marriage, and the believing husband brings holiness to his marriage."

I CORINTHIANS 7:14 (NLT)

I pray each of my children would bring holiness to their marriage relationship through their words, attitudes, and actions.

JULY 27

**"But while knowledge makes us feel important, it is love
that strengthens..."**

1 CORINTHIANS 8:1 (NLT)

I pray each of my children would realize that love is the most important thing.
I pray they would not look to knowledge to feel important, but that they
would exemplify the love of Christ in every area of their lives.

JULY 28

"We would rather put up with anything than be an obstacle to the Good News about Christ."

1 CORINTHIANS 9:12 (NLT)

I pray none of my children would ever be an obstacle to the Good News about
Christ. I pray you would strengthen them to put up with anything so that
they would be instruments of your grace.

JULY 29

**"I don't just do what is best for me; I do what is best for
others so that many may be saved."**

1 CORINTHIANS 10:33 (NLT)

I pray each of my children would look to do what is best for others, not only
for themselves, so that many may be saved.

July 30

"But if we would examine ourselves…"

1 Corinthians 11:31 (NLT)

I pray each of my children would slow down and take the time to examine themselves. I pray they would be sensitive to your Spirit as you point out sin to them and lead them to repentance.

July 31

"A spiritual gift is given to each of us so we can help each other."

1 Corinthians 12:7 (NLT)

I pray each of my children would identify, develop, and use the spiritual gifts you have given them. I pray they would consistently use their spiritual gifts to help others.

August 1

"Love never gives up, never loses faith, is always hopeful, and endures through every circumstance."

1 Corinthians 13:7 (NLT)

I pray my children would daily choose to love. I pray your love would fill them and flow from them. I pray they would never give up, never lose faith, always be hopeful, and endure through every circumstance.

AUGUST 2

"Let love be your highest goal!"

1 CORINTHIANS 14:1 (NLT)

I pray the highest goal of each of my children would be love – love for Jesus, love in their families, love in their relationships, love in their jobs, love in their ministries. Give them wisdom and courage to make love their highest goal.

AUGUST 3

"...and you still stand firm in it."

1 CORINTHIANS 15:1 (NLT)

I pray each of my children would still stand firm in the Gospel today. I pray you would strengthen and encourage them on difficult days. I pray you would reveal yourself to them on days of doubt. I pray each day of their lives they would stand firm in you.

AUGUST 4

"Be on guard. Stand firm in the faith. Be courageous. Be strong."

1 CORINTHIANS 16:13 (NLT)

I pray each of my children would live their lives on guard – on guard for the schemes of the enemy and on guard for the temptations of the world. I pray they would stand firm in their faith, they would take courage, and they would be strong. Thank you for the victory you give for their lives.

AUGUST 5

"He comforts us in all our troubles so that we can comfort others."

2 CORINTHIANS 1:4 (NLT)

Thank you that you comfort each of my children in all their troubles. I pray they would turn to you when seeking comfort and not to any false sources of comfort. Please use their troubles to prepare and strengthen them to comfort others.

AUGUST 6

"Now he uses us to spread the knowledge of Christ everywhere, like a sweet perfume."

2 CORINTHIANS 2:14 (NLT)

I pray you would use each of my children to spread the knowledge of Christ everywhere, like a sweet perfume. Do whatever you need to do in their lives so you can use them for this purpose.

AUGUST 7

**"And the Lord—who is the Spirit—makes us more
and more like him as we are changed into his
glorious image."**

2 CORINTHIANS 3:18 (NLT)

I pray you would make each of my children more and more like you as you change them into your glorious image. Thank you for the power and freedom your Spirit brings to their lives.

AUGUST 8

**"So we don't look at the troubles we can see now; rather,
we fix our gaze on things that cannot be seen. For the
things we see now will soon be gone, but the things we
cannot see will last forever."**

2 CORINTHIANS 4:18 (NLT)

I pray each of my children will daily fix their gaze on the unseen things of your kingdom. Let them see beyond the troubles and suffering of today to the purpose and plan of your heart. Let them see the truth and beauty of the things that will last forever.

AUGUST 9

"Instead, they will live for Christ, who died and was raised for them."

2 CORINTHIANS 5:15 (NLT)

I pray each of my children will daily live for Christ. I pray they remember Christ died and was raised for them. Let this knowledge direct their lives.

AUGUST 10

"We live in such a way that no one will stumble because of us…"

2 CORINTHIANS 6:3 9 (NLT)

I pray each of my children will daily live in such a way that no one will stumble because of them. Give them wisdom, strength, and courage to live what they believe.

AUGUST 11

"Because we have these promises, dear friends, let us cleanse ourselves from everything that can defile our body or spirit. And let us work toward complete holiness because we fear God."

2 CORINTHIANS 7:1 (NLT)

Thank you for the promises you have given to my children. I pray that each one will daily cleanse themselves from everything that can defile their body or spirit. Let them fear you and choose humility, righteousness, and obedience daily. Thank you for what you are doing in each of their lives.

AUGUST 12

"I want you to excel also in this gracious act of giving."

2 CORINTHIANS 8:7 (NLT)

I pray each of my children would excel in the gracious act of giving. Open their eyes to see the needs around them. Prompt them to give. Develop a generous spirit within them. Bless them and provide for them as they become channels of generosity.

AUGUST 13

**"And God will generously provide all you need. Then
you will always have everything you need and plenty left
over to share with others."**

2 CORINTHIANS 9:8 (NLT)

Thank you for generously providing everything my children need. Thank
you that you do so abundantly so they have plenty left over to share. I pray
you would open the eyes of each of my children to see their abundance. Please
develop a spirit and practice of generosity in each of their lives.

AUGUST 14

"...we hope that your faith will grow."

2 CORINTHIANS 10:15 (NLT)

I pray the faith of each of my children will daily grow. Let them recognize
your presence in their lives and your hand at work in them. Grow their roots
deep and strong in you.

AUGUST 15

"But I fear that somehow your pure and undivided devotion to Christ will be corrupted, just as Eve was deceived by the cunning ways of the serpent."

2 CORINTHIANS 11:3 9 (NLT)

Thank you that you are jealous for my children. I pray each one would live a life of pure and undivided devotion to Christ. Please protect their faith from being corrupted and keep their hearts and minds from being deceived by the enemy.

AUGUST 16

"My grace is all you need. My power works best in weakness."

2 CORINTHIANS 12:9 (NLT)

Thank you for the daily grace you provide for each of my children. Thank you that your power works best in their weakness. Please open their eyes and minds to see and understand the truth of your grace and power in their lives.

AUGUST 17

**"Be joyful. Grow to maturity. Encourage each other.
Live in harmony and peace. Then the God of love and
peace will be with you."**

2 CORINTHIANS 13:11 (NLT)

I pray each of my children will be joyful and that they will grow to maturity – physically, spiritually, mentally, and emotionally. I pray they would live in harmony and peace with each other, and with the people you place in their lives. Please establish in each one the habit of encouraging one another. Thank you that you will always be with them.

AUGUST 18

**"And now the word of the Lord is ringing out from you
to people everywhere…"**

1 THESSALONIANS 1:8 9 (NLT)

I pray the word of the Lord will take root in the hearts and lives of each of my children early in their lives, and that it would ring out from them to people everywhere.

AUGUST 19

"Our purpose is to please God, not people. He alone examines the motives of our hearts."

1 THESSALONIANS 2:4 (NLT)

I pray each of my children would live their lives with the purpose of pleasing you, not people. I pray as you examine their hearts that you find lives that are motivated by love for you and a desire to honor you in all they do and say.

AUGUST 20

"May he, as a result, make your hearts strong, blameless, and holy as you stand before God our Father when our Lord Jesus comes again"

1 THESSALONIANS 3:13 (NLT)

I pray you would make the hearts of each of my children strong, blameless, holy, and overflowing with love, as they stand before you upon your return. Thank you that you are coming soon.

AUGUST 21

"God has called us to live holy lives, not impure lives."

1 THESSALONIANS 4:7 (NLT)

Thank you that you have called each of my children to live a holy life. Please protect them from temptation. Help them to choose purity in their relationships. Help them daily to stay away from all sexual sin.

AUGUST 22

"…honor those who are your leaders in the Lord's work."

1 THESSALONIANS 5:12 (NLT)

I pray each of my children will always honor those who are their leaders in the Lord's work. I pray they will be a source of strength and encouragement to their pastors and that they will pray for them. I pray they will lead well when you call them to lead; and that they will follow well when you call them to follow.

AUGUST 23

"…you have become an example to all the believers…"

2 THESSALONIANS 1:7 (NLT)

I pray each of my children will be examples to all believers of what it means to follow Christ wholeheartedly. Let their lives be an accurate reflection of you. Teach them to love like you love.

AUGUST 24

"Our purpose is to please God, not people. He alone examines the motives of our hearts."

2 THESSALONIANS 2:4 (NLT)

Please teach my children early in life that their purpose is to please you and not people. Teach them you are the one who examines the motives of their hearts. I pray each one would walk with you daily and bring you great pleasure.

AUGUST 25

"Night and day we pray earnestly for you, asking God to let us see you again to fill the gaps in your faith."

2 THESSALONIANS 3:10 (NLT)

Lord, please fill the gaps in the faith of each of my children. Whatever questions they have, please answer them. Whatever doubts they have, please encourage them. Whatever knowledge they lack, please provide it for them. Whatever and wherever the gaps are, please meet them there.

AUGUST 26

"Don't let them waste their time in endless discussion of myths and spiritual pedigrees. These things only lead to meaningless speculations, which don't help people live a life of faith in God."

1 TIMOTHY 1:4 (NLT)

Please keep my children from meaningless speculation, discussion of myths, and spiritual pedigrees. Help each one live a life of faith in God alone and not put their trust in their own knowledge or education.

AUGUST 27

"He gave his life to purchase freedom for everyone."

1 TIMOTHY 2:6 (NLT)

Thank you for giving your life to purchase freedom for my children. I pray each one would live with the knowledge of the freedom they have in Christ. Help them see the power they have to destroy any chains or strongholds in their lives.

AUGUST 28

"They must exercise self-control and be faithful in everything they do."

1 TIMOTHY 3:11 (NLT)

Please submerge each of my children in your spirit giving them power to daily exercise self-control and to be faithful in everything they do. Please shine out through each one.

AUGUST 29

"Don't let anyone think less of you because you are young. Be an example to all believers in what you say, in the way you live, in your love, your faith, and your purity."

1 TIMOTHY 4:12 (NLT)

I pray no one would think less of my children because they are young. I pray each one would be an example to all believers in what they say, the way they live, in their love, their faith, and their purity. May each one be an example to everyone who comes in contact with them.

AUGUST 30

"Do not share in the sins of others. Keep yourself pure."

1 TIMOTHY 5:22 (NLT)

Please keep each of my children from sharing in the sins of others. Give them wisdom in choosing friends; and give them wisdom and strength to choose purity.

AUGUST 31

**"For the love of money is the root of all kinds of evil.
And some people, craving money, have wandered
from the true faith and pierced themselves with many
sorrows."**

1 TIMOTHY 6:10 (NLT)

I pray each of my children would find true wealth in godliness and contentment. Please let them never be deceived by an ungodly desire for money. Don't let them wander from true faith or be pierced by sorrows due to love of money. Give them wisdom to manage their finances in a way that honors you. Teach them to have a generous spirit. Thank you.

SEPTEMBER 1

"...fan into flames the spiritual gift God gave you..."

2 TIMOTHY 1:6 (NLT)

I pray each of my children will fan into flames the spiritual gifts that God has given them. Teach them to use those gifts for your purposes and for your glory.

SEPTEMBER 2

"A servant of the Lord must not quarrel but must be kind to everyone, be able to teach, and be patient with difficult people."

2 TIMOTHY 2:24 (NLT)

I pray my children would not be argumentative. Help them to avoid foolish talk. I pray each one would be able to teach; and they would daily choose to be patient with difficult people.

SEPTEMBER 3

"You have been taught the Holy Scriptures from childhood, and they have given you the wisdom to receive the salvation that comes by trusting in Christ Jesus."

2 TIMOTHY 3:15 (NLT)

I pray each of my children would be faithful to the things they have been taught. Please open the eyes of their hearts to see truth so they won't be deceived by the enemy. Protect them from evil people and teachers who are imposters.

SEPTEMBER 4

"But you should keep a clear mind in every situation.
Don't be afraid of suffering for the Lord. Work at telling
others the Good News, and fully carry out the ministry
God has given you."

2 TIMOTHY 4:5 (NLT)

I pray each of my children would keep a clear mind in every situation, and
they would not be afraid of suffering for the Lord. I pray each one will daily
work at telling others the Good News, and fully carry out the ministry God
has given them.

SEPTEMBER 5

"Everything is pure to those whose hearts are pure."

TITUS 1:15 (NLT)

Please create a pure heart in each of my children. I pray they would lead
blameless lives – faithful to their spouses, not arrogant or quick tempered,
dishonest or rebellious. Let them love what is good and encourage others.

SEPTEMBER 6

"And we are instructed to turn from godless living and sinful pleasures. We should live in this evil world with wisdom, righteousness, and devotion to God."

TITUS 2:12 (NLT)

I pray my children would daily turn from sinful pleasures and live a life of godliness. I pray each one would live in this world with wisdom, righteousness, and devotion to you.

SEPTEMBER 7

"He generously poured out the Spirit upon us through Jesus Christ our Savior."

TITUS 3:6 (NLT)

Thank you for generously pouring out your Spirit upon each of my children. Thank you that your spirit counsels them, convicts them, teaches them, consoles them, leads them, and empowers them. Please help each one to live in the knowledge of your Spirit within them.

SEPTEMBER 8

"And I am praying that you will put into action the generosity that comes from your faith as you understand and experience all the good things we have in Christ."

PHILEMON 1:6 (NLT)

I pray each of my children will daily put generosity into action. Thank you for all the good things you have given them in Christ. Let them live with the understanding of your generosity and goodness; and let them live out their faith generously.

SEPTEMBER 9

"The Son radiates God's own glory and expresses the very character of God, and he sustains everything by the mighty power of his command."

HEBREWS 1:3 (NLT)

I pray the lives of each of my children will radiate your glory and express your character just like Jesus does. Thank you for sustaining their lives by your mighty command. Thank you for cleansing them from sin.

SEPTEMBER 10

"So we must listen very carefully to the truth we have heard, or we may drift away from it."

HEBREWS 2:1 (NLT)

I pray each of my children will listen very carefully to the truth they have heard. Help them to believe and obey the truth. Help them to incorporate your truth into their daily lives and to live by it. Please keep them from drifting away from the truth.

SEPTEMBER 11

"For if we are faithful to the end, trusting God just as firmly as when we first believed, we will share in all that belongs to Christ."

HEBREWS 3:14 (NLT)

I pray each of my children will remain faithful to the end. I pray they will trust God just as firmly as the day they first believed. Thank you that they will share in all that belongs to Christ. Thank you for your faithfulness to complete your work in each of them.

SEPTEMBER 12

"For the word of God is alive and powerful. It is sharper
than the sharpest two-edged sword, cutting between
soul and spirit, between joint and marrow. It exposes our
innermost thoughts and desires."

HEBREWS 4:12 (NLT)

I pray you would give each of my children a deep love for your word. I pray
they would study it, believe it, practice it, proclaim it, and treasure it. Teach
them to hide your word in their hearts. Let them learn of and understand the
power of your word.

SEPTEMBER 13

"While Jesus was here on earth, he offered prayers and
pleadings, with a loud cry and tears, to the one who
could rescue him from death. And God heard his prayers
because of his deep reverence for God."

HEBREWS 5:7 (NLT)

I pray each of my children would learn to pray like Jesus. I pray they would
recognize you are the one who rescues them from death, and that they would
offer prayers and pleadings to you with loud cries, tears, and deep reverence.
Thank you for hearing and answering their prayers.

SEPTEMBER 14

"Then you will not become spiritually dull and indifferent. Instead, you will follow the example of those who are going to inherit God's promises because of their faith and endurance."

HEBREWS 6:12 (NLT)

Please protect each of my children from becoming spiritually dull or indifferent. Let them follow the example of those who are going to inherit your promises. Let them demonstrate faith and endurance every day and in every circumstance.

SEPTEMBER 15

"...He lives forever to intercede with God on their behalf."

HEBREWS 7:25 (NLT)

Thank you that Jesus lives forever to intercede with God on behalf of each of my children. Thank you that you will never forget my children. Thank you that you know each of them intimately and know perfectly how to intercede for their good. Thank you for the gift and miracle of Jesus' intercession!

SEPTEMBER 16

"...I will put my laws in their minds, and I will write them on their hearts. I will be their God, and they will be my people."

HEBREWS 8:10 (NLT)

Please put your laws in the minds of each of my children; write them on their hearts. Teach them to live according to your laws. Thank you that you are their God and that they are your people.

SEPTEMBER 17

"...For Christ died to set them free from the penalty of the sins they had committed..."

HEBREWS 9:15 (NLT)

Thank you for the sacrifice you made to set each of my children free from the penalty of their sins. Thank you for your love for each one of my children. Thank you for calling them and convicting them of sin. Thank you for setting them free.

SEPTEMBER 18

"...let us go right into the presence of God with sincere hearts fully trusting him."

HEBREWS 10:22 (NLT)

I pray each of my children would daily live in your presence with sincere hearts. I pray they would choose to trust you. I pray they would hold firmly to the hope they have in you and to your great promises. Thank you that you keep the promises you've made to them. Thank you that you can be trusted.

SEPTEMBER 19

"All these people earned a good reputation because of their faith..."

HEBREWS 11:39 (NLT)

I pray each of my children would earn a good reputation because of their faith. I pray that by faith they would accomplish every good work you have planned for each of them. I pray when they come to the end of their lives they would still be holding on to the truth of your word, and they would be remembered for their faithfulness to you.

September 20

> "Therefore, since we are surrounded by such a huge crowd of witnesses to the life of faith, let us strip off every weight that slows us down, especially the sin that so easily trips us up. And let us run with endurance the race God has set before us."

Hebrews 12:1 (NLT)

Please convict each of my children of sin and empower them to choose righteousness. Give them the strength and desire to strip off everything that slows them down in their spiritual lives. Let them learn from those who have gone before them and be encouraged to endure. Thank you for the path you have chosen for each of them.

September 21

> "Give honor to marriage, and remain faithful to one another in marriage."

Hebrews 13:4 (NLT)

I pray each of my children would give honor to marriage – to their marriages and to other's. I pray they would remain faithful across the years to their spouses. Please give them the daily wisdom, patience, strength, endurance, courage, grace, and love they will need to build strong marriages that reflect your love.

September 22

"Understand this, my dear brothers and sisters: You must all be quick to listen, slow to speak, and slow to get angry."

James 1:19 (NLT)

I pray each of my children will be quick to listen, slow to speak, and slow to get angry. Help them learn early in life that anger does not produce the righteousness of God. Teach them to practice patience, grace, forgiveness, and mercy.

September 23

"So you see, faith by itself isn't enough. Unless it produces good deeds, it is dead and useless."

James 2:17 (NLT)

Please teach each of my children that faith without good deeds is not true faith; it is useless. Open their eyes to see the needs around them. Fill them with compassion for their world. Empower and encourage them to act with humility, grace, mercy, and love every day. Let their actions prove their faith.

SEPTEMBER 24

"For if we could control our tongues, we would be perfect and could also control ourselves in every other way."

JAMES 3:2 (NLT)

Please teach each of my children the power of the spoken word. Teach them to control their tongues, to choose their words carefully, to speak less and listen more. Help them see the power they have to impart mercy, grace, encouragement, strength, joy, and love through the words they speak. Teach them to be self-controlled, through the power of the Holy Spirit, in every area of their lives.

SEPTEMBER 25

"So humble yourselves before God. Resist the devil, and he will flee from you."

JAMES 4:7 (NLT)

I pray each of my children would daily humble themselves before you. Teach them to resist the devil. Let them see the enemy flee as they walk in obedience, completely relying on you.

SEPTEMBER 26

"The earnest prayer of a righteous person has great power and produces wonderful results."

JAMES 5:16 (NLT)

Please teach each of my children to be people of prayer. Teach them how to pray. Show them the power of prayer. Let them be known as people of prayer. Thank you that you daily answer their prayers.

SEPTEMBER 27

"...May God give you more and more grace and peace."

1 PETER 1:2 (NLT)

Thank you that you always give abundant grace and peace to each of my children. I pray that you would daily give each of them the grace they need as they interact with the people in their lives, and the peace they need to walk through the circumstances of their lives. Thank you.

SEPTEMBER 28

"So get rid of all evil behavior. Be done with all deceit, hypocrisy, jealousy, and all unkind speech."

1 PETER 2:1 (NLT)

I pray each of my children would get rid of all evil behavior, that they would be done with all deceit, hypocrisy, jealousy, and unkind speech. Let them be accurate reflections of you on a daily basis in all they do and say.

SEPTEMBER 29

"...Be tenderhearted, and keep a humble attitude."

1 PETER 3:8 (NLT)

Please teach each of my children to be tenderhearted toward others. Help them to love others, and to maintain a humble attitude. Protect them from the destruction that pride brings.

September 30

**"You won't spend the rest of your lives chasing your own
desires, but you will be anxious to do the will of God."**

1 Peter 4:2 (NLT)

I pray that each of my children will spend the rest of their lives chasing the will of God. Let them see the futility of chasing their own desires, and daily choose to do your will.

October 1

**"And all of you, dress yourselves in humility as you
relate to one another…"**

1 Peter 5:5 (NLT)

I pray that each of my children would daily dress themselves in humility. Help them to walk in humility, act with humility, speak with humility, and listen in humility. Let all their relationships be characterized by humility of spirit. Thank you that you have promised grace to the humble. Please pour that grace on each of my children.

OCTOBER 2

"And because of his glory and excellence, he has given
us great and precious promises. These are the promises
that enable you to share his divine nature and escape the
world's corruption caused by human desires."

2 PETER 1:4 (NLT)

Thank you for the great and precious promises you have given to each of my children. I pray each one would respond to your promises so they can share in your divine nature and escape the corruption of the world. Thank you that you always keep your promises to them.

OCTOBER 3

"...there will be false teachers among you."

2 PETER 2:1 (NLT)

Please protect each of my children from the false teachers among us. Let your spirit within them guide them to discern what is true and what is false. Teach them to hide your word in their hearts so they will recognize truth and lies. Make them sensitive to you, to your spirit, and to your word.

OCTOBER 4

"And so, dear friends, while you are waiting for these things to happen, make every effort to be found living peaceful lives that are pure and blameless in his sight."

2 PETER 3:14 (NLT)

I pray each of my children would make every effort to live peaceful lives. I pray on the day of your return they will be found pure and blameless in your sight. I pray each one will daily grow in the grace and knowledge of Jesus.

OCTOBER 5

"And now we testify and proclaim to you that he is the one who is eternal life."

1 JOHN 1:2 (NLT)

I pray each of my children will daily testify and proclaim to everyone with whom they come in contact that Jesus is the one who is eternal life, through their words, their actions, their attitudes, and their love for others.

OCTOBER 6

"For the Spirit teaches you everything you need to know,
and what he teaches is true—it is not a lie. So just as he
has taught you, remain in fellowship with Christ."

1 JOHN 2:27 (NLT)

Please teach each of my children everything they need to know. Teach them to recognize and follow the truth on a daily basis. Lead them and help them to remain in fellowship with Christ today and every day.

OCTOBER 7

"Those who have been born into God's family do
not make a practice of sinning, because God's life is
in them."

1 JOHN 3:9 (NLT)

I pray each of my children would show they belong to God's family by the love they demonstrate to the world. Teach them to not merely say that they love, but to demonstrate that love through their attitudes, and actions. Break any practice of sin in their lives.

OCTOBER 8

"...because the Spirit who lives in you is greater than the spirit who lives in the world."

1 JOHN 4:4 (NLT)

Thank you for your Holy Spirit who lives in each of my children. Thank you that your spirit teaches them, comforts them, counsels them, convicts them, and leads them. Thank you that you enable them to recognize false teaching. Please lead them daily in the truth.

OCTOBER 9

"We know that God's children do not make a practice of sinning, for God's Son holds them securely, and the evil one cannot touch them."

1 JOHN 5:18 (NLT)

Thank you that you hold each of my children securely. Thank you that you keep the evil one from touching them. I pray each one would daily walk in the knowledge and freedom of their security in you and not make a practice of sinning.

OCTOBER 10

"Grace, mercy, and peace, which come from God the Father and from Jesus Christ—the Son of the Father—will continue to be with us who live in truth and love."

2 JOHN 1:3 (NLT)

Thank you that lasting grace, unfailing mercy, and true peace come from you. Please enable each of my children to look to you for these things. Thank you that you continue to be with my children daily. Please help them to live in truth and love.

OCTOBER 11

"I could have no greater joy than to hear that my children are following the truth."

3 JOHN 1:4 (NLT)

I pray each of my children would daily follow the truth. Thank you for the joy you give to them as they do so; and for the joy you give to me as I watch them.

OCTOBER 12

"But you, dear friends, must build each other up in your most holy faith, pray in the power of the Holy Spirit,"

JUDE 1:20 (NLT)

I pray my children would daily build each other up in their faith. Teach them to pray in the power of the Holy Spirit. Thank you for the influence they have on one another, and let them use that influence for your kingdom.

OCTOBER 13

"But you will receive power when the Holy Spirit comes upon you."

ACTS 1:8 (NLT)

Thank you that you have given your Holy Spirit to each of my children. Thank you that your Spirit empowers them on a daily basis. Please help them to live in the knowledge and awareness of your Spirit at work in their lives. Help them to submit to the work of your Spirit in their lives. Empower them to be your witnesses at home and around the world.

OCTOBER 14

"Then Peter stepped forward..."

ACTS 2:14 (NLT)

I pray each of my children would have the courage to daily step forward for Christ. I pray they would boldly share their faith, humbly walk in step with you, generously give, and selflessly serve each person they meet. Help them to step forward in their relationships, in their jobs, and in every area of their lives.

OCTOBER 15

"Now repent of your sins and turn to God, so that your sins may be wiped away."

ACTS 3:19 (NLT)

Please convict each of my children of sin. As you do, I pray they would repent of that sin and turn back to you. Thank you for your faithfulness to wipe their sins away.

OCTOBER 16

"They also recognized them as men who had been with Jesus."

ACTS 4:13 (NLT)

I pray each of my children will be recognized as men and women who have been with Jesus. Please give them great boldness to tell everything they know about you. May miraculous signs and wonders and healings be done through their lives and ministries.

OCTOBER 17

"And every day, in the Temple and from house to house, they continued to teach and preach this message: "Jesus is the Messiah."

ACTS 5:42 (NLT)

I pray each of my children will daily continue to preach and teach, with their words and with their actions, that Jesus is the Messiah, in the church, in their communities, and in their homes.

OCTOBER 18

"At this point everyone in the high council stared at Stephen, because his face became as bright as an angel's."

ACTS 6:15 (NLT)

Please help each of my children to be an accurate reflection of you. I pray that when people see my children, they see you. Let their faces be as bright as an angel's.

OCTOBER 19

"But Stephen, full of the Holy Spirit, gazed steadily into heaven and saw the glory of God, and he saw Jesus standing in the place of honor at God's right hand."

ACTS 7:55 (NLT)

I pray each of my children would daily gaze steadily into heaven. I pray that they would see the glory of God at work, and they would recognize the place of honor that Jesus holds. Help them daily maintain their focus on Jesus.

OCTOBER 20

"He preached the Good News there and in every town along the way..."

ACTS 8:40 (NLT)

I pray each of my children would live their lives in such a way that the Good News is proclaimed in every town along the way. Let their daily actions, words, and attitudes shine a light on the Good News of your love and salvation.

OCTOBER 21

"Who are you, Lord?"

ACTS 9:5 (NLT)

Please draw each of my children to you. Give them a strong desire to know who you are. Let them daily ask the question, "Who are you, Lord?" and please clearly answer, showing them your holiness, grace, and goodness. Thank you that you let them know you.

OCTOBER 22

"...the Holy Spirit fell upon all who were listening to the message."

ACTS 10:44 (NLT)

I pray your Holy Spirit will fall upon each of my children on a daily basis. Let your Spirit fill them, cleanse them, instruct them, lead them, empower them and flow from them to everyone they come in contact.

OCTOBER 23

"The Holy Spirit told me to go…"

ACTS 11:12 (NLT)

Please lead each of my children by your Holy Spirit. I pray each one would be sensitive to your voice. I pray they would daily follow you whenever and wherever you tell them to go. Thank you that you go before them and you go with them. Thank you that as they follow the leading of your Spirit they will see your hand at work.

OCTOBER 24

"The Lord has sent his angel and saved me from Herod…"

ACTS 12:11 (NLT)

Thank you for your daily protection of my children. Thank you that you are watching and you are aware of the dangers and schemes of the enemy against them. Thank you that you daily place angels around each of them, you guide their steps as they follow you, and you always provide a way of escape.

OCTOBER 25

"But he is coming soon—and I'm not even worthy to be his slave and untie the sandals on his feet."

ACTS 13:25 (NLT)

I pray each of my children would daily live in light of the reality that Jesus will return. Teach them to clearly see Jesus' position as Sovereign Lord and King and yet understand his unconditional, uncontainable, unstoppable love for them.

OCTOBER 26

"They encouraged them to continue in the faith, reminding them that we must suffer many hardships to enter the Kingdom of God."

ACTS 14:22 (NLT)

Please bring people into the lives of my children who will encourage them to continue in the faith. Let each of my children encourage others to continue in their faith. I pray you would remind them that suffering is expected as they follow Christ. Give them the grace they need to walk through that suffering.

OCTOBER 27

"God knows people's hearts…"

ACTS 15:8 (NLT)

Thank you that you know the heart of each of my children. Thank you that you know their thoughts, desires, dreams, fears, and motives. Please continue the work you have begun in each of their hearts. Let their hearts be faithful to you daily.

OCTOBER 28

"Paul wanted to take him along on the journey…"

ACTS 16:3 (NIV)

I pray each of my children would take others along with them on the journey. I pray they would live in such a way they would attract others to your Kingdom. I pray they would daily be light in the darkness to show others the way.

OCTOBER 29

"As was his custom, Paul went into the synagogue…"

ACTS17:2 (NIV)

I pray each of my children would develop habits in their lives that would draw them deeper and closer to you. I pray they would develop regular habits of prayer, study and memorization of your Word, corporate worship, fellowship with other believers, and daily time alone with you. Develop in each of them the habit of sharing their faith through their lives. Teach them the value and power of habits.

OCTOBER 30

"Every Sabbath he reasoned in the synagogue, trying to persuade Jews and Greeks."

ACTS 18:4 (NIV)

I pray each of my children would be found in church every week. I pray they would use their voices to reason, teach, lead, worship, love, encourage, strengthen, and persuade others to come into relationship with Christ.

OCTOBER 31

"God did extraordinary miracles through Paul,"

ACTS 19:11 (NIV)

Please do extraordinary miracles through each of my children. Let their lives be a living example of your power, your goodness, and your love for us. Open their eyes to see the daily miracles you are doing; and I pray they would each give thanks, honor, and glory to you for these miracles.

NOVEMBER 1

"...my only aim is to finish the race and complete the task the Lord Jesus has given me—the task of testifying to the good news of God's grace."

ACTS 20:24 (NIV)

I pray each of my children would set their only aim to finish the race and complete the task that you have given them. I pray they would daily testify to the good news of your grace; and that many would come to know you because of the lives of my children.

NOVEMBER 2

"We sought out the disciples there..."

ACTS 21:4 (NIV)

I pray each of my children would always seek out other believers in their lives. I pray they would seek believers to be their closest friends, advisors, counselors, leaders, and pastors. Open their eyes to understand the importance of other believers in their lives.

NOVEMBER 3

"I asked, 'What should I do, Lord?'"

ACTS 22:10 (NLT)

I pray each of my children would daily ask you what they should do. Please enable them to accomplish your plans for their lives on a daily basis.

NOVEMBER 4

**"The following night the Lord stood near Paul and said,
'Take courage!'..."**

ACTS 23:11 (NIV)

Thank you for standing near to each of my children. Thank you for never leaving them. Thank you for daily whispering to their hearts, "Take courage!" I pray each of my children would hear your voice and be encouraged by your presence, your peace, your strength, and your love.

NOVEMBER 5

**"So I strive always to keep my conscience clear before
God and man."**

ACTS 24:16 (NIV)

I pray each of my children would daily strive to keep a clear conscience before God and man. I pray each one would live their life in such a way that those who don't know you find you in them.

NOVEMBER 6

"They brought many serious charges against him, but they could not prove them."

ACTS 25:7 (NIV)

I pray any time the enemy comes against my children with false accusations, they would stand strong in their faith. Please give each of them strength and courage to stand for your truth and justice. Help them to identify the lies of the enemy and to daily live and act in your truth.

NOVEMBER 7

"Now get to your feet! For I have appeared to you to appoint you as my servant and witness."

ACTS 26:16 (NLT)

Please develop in the hearts of my children a desire to be your servants and your witnesses. Wherever their feet may take them, let them always bear witness of who you are and what you've done for them.

NOVEMBER 8

"Julius, in kindness to Paul, allowed him to go to his friends so they might provide for his needs."

ACTS 27:3 (NIV)

Thank you for the faithful friends you have provided for each of my children. I pray each one would be the same – a faithful friend. I pray they would always seek to provide for the needs of their friends. I pray they would be the one their friends turn to in good times and bad. Let them be salt and light in the lives of their friends.

NOVEMBER 9

"He proclaimed the kingdom of God and taught about the Lord Jesus Christ—with all boldness and without hindrance!"

ACTS 28:31 (NIV)

Please give your boldness to each of my children to proclaim your Kingdom and to tell about Jesus. I pray you would remove anything in their lives that would hinder them from proclaiming your goodness. Convict them of sin, lead them to repentance, so that their testimony will be seen, heard, and believed.

NOVEMBER 10

"For although they knew God, they neither glorified
him as God nor gave thanks to him, but their thinking
became futile and their foolish hearts were darkened."

ROMANS 1:21 (NIV)

I pray each of my children would daily glorify you and give you thanks. Open
their eyes to the power of worship and gratitude. Protect each one from futility of thought and foolishness of heart.

NOVEMBER 11

"You, therefore, have no excuse, you who pass judgment
on someone else, for at whatever point you judge another, you are condemning yourself, because you who pass
judgment do the same things."

ROMANS 2:1 (NIV)

Please teach each of my children to offer love and grace in place of judgment.
Help them always seek to understand and know the stories of the people in
their lives. Convict them of the sin of self-righteousness.

NOVEMBER 12

"and all are justified freely by his grace through the redemption that came by Christ Jesus."

ROMANS 3:24 (NIV)

Thank you for freely giving your grace to each of my children. Thank you that you have justified each one before you. Let them daily see your power and grace at work in their lives. Teach them to depend on you alone.

NOVEMBER 13

"Yet he did not waver through unbelief regarding the promise of God, but was strengthened in his faith and gave glory to God,"

ROMANS 4:20 (NIV)

I pray none of my children will waver through unbelief regarding your promises. Please give them courage and strength to stand on your promises even when they can't see your hand at work. I pray they will be daily strengthened in their faith and that they will daily give glory to you.

NOVEMBER 14

"...but we also glory in our sufferings, because we know that suffering produces perseverance;"

ROMANS 5:3 (NIV)

I pray each of my children would learn to glory in their sufferings. I pray none of their sufferings would go to waste. Please use their sufferings to produce perseverance, character, and hope in each one of them.

NOVEMBER 15

"We are those who have died to sin; how can we live in it any longer?"

ROMANS 6:2 (NIV)

Thank you for the sacrifice you made for each of my children so they could experience forgiveness and freedom from sin. I pray each one would live in that freedom on a daily basis. Open the eyes of their hearts to see that they are dead to sin and no longer have to live enslaved to the power of sin in their lives. Help each one to daily choose righteousness.

NOVEMBER 16

"For in my inner being I delight in God's law;"

ROMANS 7:22 (NIV)

Thank you for the power of your resurrection living in each of my children. I pray they would learn that sin no longer has power in their lives as their spirits delight in your law. Please break through any stronghold of sin in their lives. Help each one to daily live in your victory.

NOVEMBER 17

"Therefore, there is now no condemnation for those who are in Christ Jesus,"

ROMANS 8:1 (NIV)

Thank you that you provided for the salvation of each of my children. Thank you they now live a life of freedom and not a life of condemnation. Thank you that nothing will ever separate them from your love – nothing. Teach each one to walk in new life, filled with your Spirit

NOVEMBER 18

"It does not, therefore, depend on human desire or effort, but on God's mercy."

ROMANS 9:16 (NIV)

Thank you that the salvation of my children does not depend on their desire or effort, but completely on your mercy. Thank you that your grace and mercy cover every sin in their lives. Thank you that every good thing in their lives and every victory come as a result of your mercy.

NOVEMBER 19

"As Scripture says, 'Anyone who believes in him will never be put to shame.'"

ROMANS 10:11 (NIV)

Thank you that because my children believe in you and your word, they will never be put to shame. Please give each one confidence in you and your word. Please give each one courage to boldly declare your Gospel with their words, attitudes, and actions.

NOVEMBER 20

"For from him and through him and for him are all things. To him be the glory forever!"

ROMANS 11:36 (NIV)

I pray each of my children would recognize everything they have comes from you. Remind them that nothing can come into their lives that hasn't first come through you. Help them daily live their lives for you, and to give you glory forever.

NOVEMBER 21

"Do not conform to the pattern of this world, but be transformed by the renewing of your mind."

ROMANS 12:2 (NIV)

I pray each of my children would daily be transformed by the renewing of their minds. Help them choose not to conform to this world. I pray they would offer their bodies as a living sacrifice, holy and pleasing to you.

NOVEMBER 22

"...whoever rebels against the authority is rebelling against what God has instituted, and those who do so will bring judgment on themselves."

ROMANS 13:2 (NIV)

Please remove any spirit of rebellion in my children. I pray each one would have an attitude of respect toward those in authority over them. I pray they would daily demonstrate respect in every relationship, and they would maintain an attitude of respect toward you and your word. Open their eyes to see the power of respect and the consequences of rebellion. Give them wisdom to choose respect and obedience.

NOVEMBER 23

"So let's stop condemning each other. Decide instead to live in such a way that you will not cause another believer to stumble and fall."

ROMANS 14:13 (NLT)

I pray each of my children would decide to live in such a way that they won't cause other believers to stumble or fall. I pray they would not judge or condemn other believers but that they would be examples for them of what it means to live a life filled with your Holy Spirit. Give them wisdom in each decision they make, knowing their lives impact the faith of others.

NOVEMBER 24

"I pray that God, the source of hope, will fill you completely with joy and peace because you trust in him. Then you will overflow with confident hope through the power of the Holy Spirit."

ROMANS 15:13 (NLT)

Please completely fill each of my children with joy and peace as they trust in you. Let them overflow with confident hope through the power of the Holy Spirit. I pray this confidence and hope would lead them to share your good news with those who have never heard your name. Let their joy and peace lead them to worship you.

NOVEMBER 25

"Watch out for people who cause divisions and upset people's faith by teaching things contrary to what you have been taught. Stay away from them."

ROMANS 16:17 (NLT)

Please protect each of my children from those who would upset their faith, from those who would teach them things that are untrue, and from those who would cause division among your church. Give them discernment to know who those people are and wisdom to stay away from them. If my children do such things, please convict them of sin and bring them back into right relationship with you.

PRAYERS FOR MY CHILDREN

NOVEMBER 26

"From his abundance we have all received one gracious blessing after another."

JOHN 1:16 (NLT)

Thank you for your unfailing love and faithfulness toward each of my children. Thank you that from your abundance they daily receive one gracious blessing after another. Thank you for the light you bring to their lives. Open the eyes of their hearts to see your love for them. I pray that others will believe because of their testimony.

NOVEMBER 27

"...Do whatever he tells you."

JOHN 2:5 (NLT)

I pray each of my children would know you so well that they trust you completely. I pray each one would do whatever you tell them, whether they understand or not, because they trust you. Teach them to hear your voice and to walk in obedience daily.

NOVEMBER 28

"He must become greater and greater, and I must become less and less."

JOHN 3:30 (NLT)

I pray you would daily become greater and greater in the lives of each of my children. I pray your life and your presence would eclipse them and that the world would see more and more of you in their lives every day.

NOVEMBER 29

"...And the man believed what Jesus said..."

JOHN 4:50 (NLT)

I pray each of my children would believe what Jesus said. I pray they would build their lives on your word, base their decisions on your word, and find strength, peace, comfort, and courage in your word. As they do so, open their eyes to see your faithfulness, power, and miracles.

NOVEMBER 30

"John was like a burning and shining lamp..."

JOHN 5:35 (NLT)

I pray each of my children will be like burning and shining lamps. I pray they would burn and shine for you. I pray that their words and actions would daily bring glory and honor to you, and that they would point others to you.

DECEMBER 1

"The Spirit alone gives eternal life. Human effort accomplishes nothing."

JOHN 6:63 (NLT)

Thank you for providing the way to eternal life for each of my children. Thank you that their salvation does not depend on their human effort but rests completely on you. Please help them to daily walk in the truth of your salvation and the power of your Spirit.

DECEMBER 2

"I want to do what is good, but I don't. I don't want to do what is wrong, but I do it anyway."

ROMANS 7:19 (NLT)

Please teach each of my children to overcome the power of sin in their lives. Show them the power they have to choose righteousness and to run from sin. Please remind them and call them daily to be filled with your Spirit and to walk in step with you. Please break down any strongholds of sin in their lives.

DECEMBER 3

"And the one who sent me is with me—he has not deserted me. For I always do what pleases him."

JOHN 8:29 (NLT)

Thank you that you are always with each of my children and you will never desert them. Thank you that you always see them, you always hear them, and you always respond to them. I pray each one would consistently choose to do what pleases you.

DECEMBER 4

"This happened so the power of God could be seen in him."

JOHN 9:3 (NLT)

I pray your power would be seen in the lives of each of my children. Let your power be seen in and through the circumstances of their lives. Help each one to trust in your heart whatever circumstances come their way, knowing that your plans for them are good and that your power will be manifest again.

DECEMBER 5

"The thief's purpose is to steal and kill and destroy. My purpose is to give them a rich and satisfying life."

JOHN 10:10 (NLT)

Thank you for your good plans for each of my children. Help them learn as they walk in step with you, you will give them a rich and satisfying life. Please protect each of them from the plans of the enemy to steal, kill, and destroy them.

DECEMBER 6

"...for now you will really believe."

JOHN 11:15 (NLT)

I pray you would provide situations, opportunities, and circumstances in the lives of each of my children that will lead them to really believe in you and in the truth of your word. Teach them to trust you even when everything seems hopeless. As they do, please pour out your grace, mercy, power, and blessing on each of their lives.

DECEMBER 7

"Anyone who wants to serve me must follow me, because my servants must be where I am."

JOHN 12:26 (NLT)

I pray each of my children would daily follow you. Give them the desire to be where you are, and open their eyes to see the necessity of doing so. I pray that in your presence they feel at home. Thank you that you will fill them with peace, joy, power, hope, and love as they remain in your presence.

DECEMBER 8

"I have given you an example to follow. Do as I have done to you."

JOHN 13:15 (NLT)

I pray each of my children would daily follow Jesus' example. I pray they would come to know you so well that following you comes easily and automatically. Please teach each one to see, hear, think, understand, speak, and act as you would. Let each one daily have the attitude of Jesus.

DECEMBER 9

"Don't let your hearts be troubled. Trust in God, and trust also in me."

JOHN 14:1 (NLT)

I pray each of my children will learn early in life that they can choose not to let their hearts be troubled. I pray they will daily choose to trust in you no matter what the circumstances look like or how they feel. Thank you for your good heart toward each one, and your good plans for their lives.

DECEMBER 10

"...and you cannot be fruitful unless you remain in me."

JOHN 15:4 (NLT)

I pray that each of my children would daily remain in you. Teach them to obey your commandments and in so doing to remain in your love. Let their lives be fruitful examples of what it means to be followers of Christ.

DECEMBER 11

"I tell you the truth, you will ask the Father directly, and he will grant your request because you use my name."

JOHN 16:23 (NLT)

Please teach my children to pray. Show them your power, grace, and faithfulness as they pray. Let prayer become their first response. Please draw them to spend daily time with you in prayer. Let them see your hand at work in response to their prayers. Let their prayer time become a time of joy and strength for each one.

DECEMBER 12

"I'm not asking you to take them out of the world, but to keep them safe from the evil one."

JOHN 17:15 (NLT)

Please help each of my children live in the knowledge that they don't belong to this world but they belong to you. I pray you would keep them safe from the evil one while they are in this world. When the world rejects, ridicules, or falsely accuses them, please remind them that they belong to you.

December 13

**"Shall I not drink from the cup of suffering the Father
has given me?"**

John 18:11 (NLT)

Please help each of my children to recognize that suffering is part of life and that they are not exempt. During times of suffering teach them to turn to you. Please use the suffering in their lives to show them who you are. I pray suffering will be a strong teacher in their lives. I pray that in the midst of suffering they will be convinced that you are good, your plans are good, and you will never leave them.

December 14

"I find him not guilty."

John 19:6 (NLT)

Thank you for sending Jesus to be the savior for each of my children. Thank you for providing the perfect sacrifice for their sins. Thank you for declaring each one not guilty as they put their trust in you. Teach each one to walk in the truth of their salvation.

DECEMBER 15

"Stop doubting and believe."

JOHN 20:27 (NIV)

Thank you that when my children have doubts you come to meet them there. Please remove any doubts they have and help each one to stop doubting and believe. Open their hearts and minds to know the truth and to trust you daily.

DECEMBER 16

**"None of the disciples dared ask him, "Who are you?"
They knew it was the Lord."**

JOHN 21:12 (NIV)

I pray each of my children would daily recognize you at work in their lives. I pray they would walk so closely with you that they immediately recognize your hand at work. I pray they would never need to ask, "Who are you?" because they clearly know it is you. Please continue to draw each one into deep intimacy with you.

DECEMBER 17

"...and they will call him Immanuel, which means 'God is with us.'"

MATTHEW 1:23 (NIV)

Thank you for your presence in the life of each of my children. Thank you that you will always be with them, you will never leave them. Thank you for the peace and security this truth brings. Help each one to rest and hope in you.

DECEMBER 18

"...and we have come to worship him."

MATTHEW 2:2 (NLT)

I pray each of my children would draw close to you today to worship you. I pray each one would develop a daily habit of worship. I pray they would find strength, peace, endurance, and hope as they worship you. Please draw them to you daily.

DECEMBER 19

"Prove by the way you live that you have repented of your sins and turned to God."

MATTHEW 3:8 (NLT)

Please develop in each of my children a sensitivity to your Spirit at work in their lives. Please convict them of sin and of truth. I pray each one will be quick to repent of their sins and turn to you. Let righteousness shine in their lives; and let their lives be proof of their relationship with you.

DECEMBER 20

"Get out of here, Satan," Jesus told him. "For the Scriptures say, 'You must worship the Lord your God and serve only him.'"

MATTHEW 4:10 (NLT)

I pray each of my children would worship the Lord our God and serve him only. Please develop wisdom and discernment in each of them so they are able to recognize the schemes of the enemy as he comes against them. Teach them to stand with you and tell the enemy to leave.

DECEMBER 21

"In the same way, let your good deeds shine out for all to see, so that everyone will praise your heavenly Father."

MATTHEW 5:16 (NLT)

I pray each of my children would let their good deeds shine out for all to see, today and every day of their lives. I pray their good deeds will point others to you and lead them to praise you. I pray my children would never be ashamed to live for you and walk in your truth.

DECEMBER 22

"Seek the Kingdom of God above all else, and live righteously, and he will give you everything you need."

MATTHEW 6:33 (NLT)

I pray each of my children will daily seek your kingdom above all else. Teach them to live righteously and to store their treasure in heaven. Thank you for your promise to give them everything they need as they make you and your kingdom the priority of their lives.

DECEMBER 23

"Yes, just as you can identify a tree by its fruit, so you can identify people by their actions."

MATTHEW 7:20 (NLT)

I pray each of my children would study and know your word, and that they would daily put it into practice in their lives. I pray they would be identified as followers of Jesus by their actions. Please continue to mature each one so they produce good fruit. I pray the fruit of the spirit would be clearly evident in each of their lives.

DECEMBER 24

"Because you believed, it has happened."

MATTHEW 8:13 (NLT)

I pray each of my children would see your miracles take place because they believe. I pray you would do miracles in their lives; and that you would do miracles through their lives. I pray their relationship with you would be so intimate that they trust you completely.

DECEMBER 25

"Be encouraged, my child! Your sins are forgiven."

MATTHEW 9:2 (NLT)

Thank you for forgiving the sins of each of my children. Help them to live in this truth. Thank you for the freedom they have because of this truth. Please daily lead them to confession and repentance of sin so they can experience the joy of your forgiveness. Let your forgiveness give them courage.

DECEMBER 26

**"If you cling to your life, you will lose it; but if you give
up your life for me, you will find it."**

MATTHEW 10:39 (NLT)

I pray each of my children would daily choose to give up their lives for You.
Thank you that as they do, they will find you and find life. In difficult times,
please remind them to cling to you.

DECEMBER 27

**"Take my yoke upon you. Let me teach you, because I
am humble and gentle at heart, and you will find rest for
your souls."**

MATTHEW 11:29 (NLT)

Thank you that each of my children will find a gentle heart and rest for their
souls when they come to you. I pray each one would recognize that truth. I
pray they would daily come to you and take up your yoke. Teach them to be
humble and gentle of heart just like you.

DECEMBER 28

**"A good person produces good things from the treasury
of a good heart, and an evil person produces evil things
from the treasury of an evil heart."**

MATTHEW 12:35 (NLT)

Please continue the work of transformation you started in each of my children. Please produce a good heart in each of them. Please develop a deep treasury in each of their hearts, and let good things from that treasury be evident in their lives daily.

DECEMBER 29

"To those who listen to my teaching, more understanding will be given, and they will have an abundance of knowledge."

MATTHEW 13:12 (NLT)

I pray each of my children would listen to your teaching. Thank you that you are the source of understanding and knowledge. Please continue to give them more understanding and an abundance of knowledge as they listen to your teaching and trust you.

DECEMBER 30

"Then they went and told Jesus what had happened."

MATTHEW 14:12 (NLT)

I pray each of my children would have such a close comfortable relationship with you that they always turn to you. I pray each one would feel like your friend, and they would come to you to share the stories of their life. Let them walk daily in friendship with you.

DECEMBER 31

"I will give you the keys of the kingdom of heaven; whatever you bind on earth will be bound in heaven, and whatever you loose on earth will be loosed in heaven."

MATTHEW 16:19 (NLT)

Thank you for giving each of my children the keys to the kingdom of heaven. Help them understand what that means and the power you have given them to impact the world around them for your kingdom. Call each one to daily take up their cross and follow you.

About the Author

Laura Shook is a teacher, speaker, and one of the founding pastors of the Community of Faith located in Cypress, Texas. Now over eight thousand people worship there each weekend. Shook is responsible for setting the tone of the international ministries for the church. With a passion for bringing awareness to global issues, Shook is particularly interested in helping illuminate issues relating to broken or forgotten individuals.

You can usually find Shook enjoying one of her many interests, including ice cream, reading, traveling, and spending time with her family. Shook is the author of *Forever Hope: Choosing Life through Cancer and Recovery*, which was published by Maida Vale Publishing in 2015.

Made in the USA
Columbia, SC
21 August 2024

40762668R00093